CLASSIC ADIRONDACK SKI TOURS

by Tony Goodwin

The Adirondack Mountain Club, Inc.

Note: ADK makes every effort to keep its guidebooks up to date, however, each printing can only be as current as the last press date; thus use of this information is at the sole risk of the user.

Reprinted with revisions 1996

Library of Congress Cataloging-in-Publication Data

Goodwin, Tony, 1949-
    Classic Adirondack Ski Tours / by Tony Goodwin.
        p.   cm.
    Includes index.
    ISBN 0-935272-67-4 : $10.95
        1. Cross-country skiing—New York (State)—Adirondack Mountains-
    -Guidebooks. 2. Adirondack Mountains (N.Y.)—Guidebooks.
    I. Title.
    GV854.5.A25G66   1994
    796.93'2'097475—dc20   93-23288
                                                                            CIP

Printed in the United States of America

10 9 8 7 6 5 4 3 2   96 97 98 99

This book is dedicated to

Almy Coggeshall

who was writing about how and where to cross-country ski long before many of us took our first stride.

A leader of ski tours for many years, Almy wrote an instructional book, *Ski Touring in the Northeastern United States* (1965), plus two guidebooks: *Nordic Skiing Trails in New York State* (1977) and *25 Ski Tours in the Adirondacks* (1979). Although the equipment has changed in appearance over the past 30 years and these books are now out of print, Almy's descriptions of how to glide through the winter landscape are as good as any that exist in print today. His two guidebooks were the first to introduce many of the tours described in this book.

ACKNOWLEDGMENTS

Though bearing the name of a single author, the production of this guidebook has been a cooperative effort on the part of all the authors of the guidebooks in the Adirondack Mountain Club's Forest Preserve series. The author would therefore like to sincerely thank Linda Laing, Arthur W. Haberl, Carl Heilman, Peter O'Shea, and Bruce Wadsworth both for their contributions in selecting the tours to be included and for their comments on the manuscript as it progressed toward publication. Thanks are also due to Karen Brooks of the Adirondack Mountain Club staff who put in many additional hours to produce the page maps that accompany each description. Finally, the work you now hold in your hand would not have been published without the efforts of Andrea Masters and Robin Richards of the Adirondack Mountain Club's publications staff who converted the manuscript into a finished work.

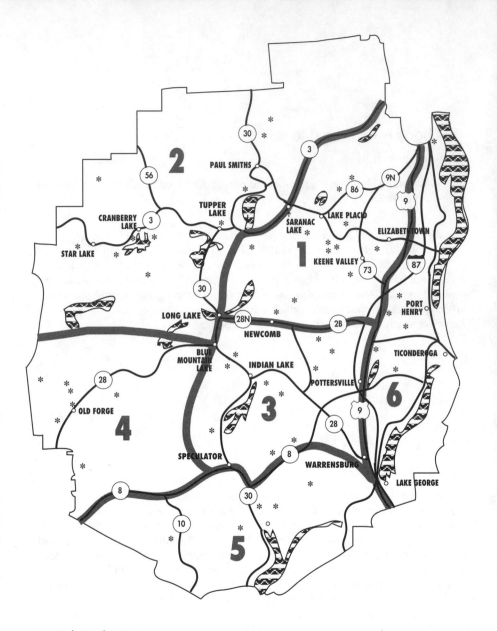

1 High Peaks Region
2 Northern Region
3 Central Region
4 West-Central Region
5 Southern Region
6 Eastern Region
* Tours described in this guide

CONTENTS

INTRODUCTION

The Adirondacks offer practically limitless opportunities for cross-country skiing, and the past twenty years have seen a tremendous interest in exploring these many and varied possibilities. In the early eighties, two ski-touring guides described a number of the cross-country ski trips then being done; both are now out of print, and much has been learned since then as the sport has continued to grow in spite of a series of low snow winters. The past ten years have also seen the Adirondack Mountain Club complete a comprehensive series of hiking guides for the entire Adirondack Park. This present guide draws both on the knowledge gained by skiers over the past two decades and on the information contained in the ADK hiking guide series. It offers a good sampling from among the many possible cross-country ski trips in the Adirondacks.

The trips are arranged by regions corresponding to those covered by the ADK hiking guides. A brief introduction to each region gives information on the type of terrain offered, a list of cross-country ski centers, and possible sources of information on the current ski conditions.

CROSS-COUNTRY SKIING IN THE ADIRONDACKS

This guide assumes that its users are at least moderately experienced and can recognize both their skiing ability in relation to different types of terrain and their limits as to distances to be covered. It makes no attempt to teach one how to ski or how to select all of the equipment necessary for an extended trip.

Aside from the potential of being far more remote, Adirondack skiing is much like the skiing in other mountainous areas of the northeast. The weather can be severe at times, with sudden 30- to 40-degree drops in temperature (°F) possible at any time during the winter; a warm spell with rain can be followed by colder weather and treacherous crust; and a heavy fall of snow can slow one's pace to a near crawl and necessitate a change of plans. Do not set out with the idea that the temperature and conditions will remain the same all day and always have an alternate plan in the event that the proposed trip is not feasible.

Emergency Gear

None of the trips described in this guide are patrolled, so you are on your own as far as safety and rescue are concerned. On the longer trips especially, each skier should carry enough clothing to keep warm for an extended period of inactivity in the event that an injury forces the group to stop. One should also carry enough to stay alive (though not necessarily comfortable) if forced to spend the night. Additionally, someone in the party should have an extra ski tip, a few tools to repair broken equipment, a foam pad to insulate any injured person from the snow, and a tarp or space blanket. Though bulky to carry, a sleeping bag is desirable as it can be many hours before help arrives. A bit of plumber's tape, a few radiator hose clamps, some wire, and some nylon cord are also useful both for field repair of equipment and for constructing a makeshift toboggan on which to move an injured skier.

Backcountry rescues are the responsibility of the Department of Environmental Conservation Forest Rangers. Names and phone numbers of the local rangers are posted at major trailheads or can be found in the phone book under "New York, State of"; "Environmental Conservation, Department of." If you cannot locate a forest ranger, call the State Police. They will be able to find someone in the DEC who can help.

Equipment

Skis: On all of the trips described one should expect unbroken snow and no prepared tracks. "Racing" or "training" skis are not appropriate, but all the described trips can, and commonly are, done on either "light touring" or "touring" skis. While some may prefer the extra control and flotation of "mountain" skis with metal edges, the trade-off is that these heavier, wider skis make for slower progress on the easier terrain. Very wide "bushwhacker" type skis have recently become popular with some skiers, but these are very slow on flatter sections. Furthermore, in deep, unbroken snow anyone with such wide skis will be expected to break trail the entire distance—unless, of course, everyone in the party has the same skis.

Poles: Avoid poles with small, racing-style baskets; otherwise any sturdy touring pole will do.

Boots: On extended trips warmth is perhaps the most important consideration, followed by control and support. While the technology likely will continue to evolve, the boots that still best meet the above criteria are the old favorite 75mm, three-pin boots. A boot that comes up at least to the ankle is preferred, with gaiters and overboots added for additional warmth if needed .

Clothing: Volumes have been written about the merits of various types of winter clothing, but the one common thread is that cotton is to be avoided. Synthetic pile or wool are desirable because they do not soak up water and retain most of their insulating capability even when wet. A windproof outer layer is also important—especially if the proposed trip includes any open areas such as summits or lakes.

SNOWFALL AND SNOW CONDITIONS

Unlike their downhill counterparts who have come to expect "power-tilled" boulevards of man-made snow as practically standard-issue conditions, cross-country skiers often must do a good deal of planning and thinking to find a suitable trip with the right snow conditions.

Amounts: Snowfall amounts can vary tremendously from one part of the Adirondacks to another. The western and southern edges generally receive more snow than the northern and eastern areas. Average annual snowfall at Old Forge, for instance, is between 180 and 200 inches, tailing off to 150 inches at Blue Mt. Lake, Cranberry Lake, Northville, and Newcomb. North Creek and Paul Smiths average around 120 inches, while the Lake Placid area averages just over 100 inches. The Champlain Valley and much of the eastern Adirondacks receive from 70 to 90 inches.

These differences are most apparent in low snow years when areas such as Old Forge, Newcomb, Paul Smiths, or Northville might have passably good conditions while most of the rest of the northeast has virtually no snow at all. It pays to call around: it has been rare that on any given winter's day at least a few of the trips in this book have not been skiable.

The other significant factor in snowfall is elevation. Areas above 2,000 feet receive considerably more snow, and above 3,000 feet the difference in snow depth can be pronounced—up to more than one foot for each 1,000 feet of additional elevation. Most skiers consider this gain in snow depth an advantage, but remember that more snow also means slower trailbreaking.

Conditions: While fresh powder is nice, skiers should be prepared for the full range of conditions and the possibility that things can change even during the course of an afternoon tour. The difficulty rating for each trip assumes either cold powder or soft, corn snow conditions. Icy conditions naturally raise the difficulty of a given trip. Breakable crust may make a trip practically impossible and certainly not very enjoyable.

Travel on Ice: Several of the trips described in this guide cross lakes, and it must be each skier's own judgment at the time whether the ice is safe. Be aware that after a major thaw even seemingly thick ice can be dangerously weak, and be especially cautious near inlets and outlets of lakes at any time.

Another problem on lakes is that sometimes water will seep up through cracks in the ice and create a layer of slush under the snow that will freeze on any ski. The lead skier may often skim over these areas, but following skiers should watch for gray areas forming in the tracks and ski around them. Carry a good scraper (and possibly an extra in case someone in the party has forgotten) so that the group can resume movement as soon as possible in the event that everyone ices up.

Public and Private Land: Of the more than six million acres contained within the "Blue Line" of the Adirondack Park, only about forty percent is actually owned by the State of New York. This 2,400,000 acres of public land comprises the Adirondack Forest Preserve and since 1896 has been constitutionally protected to remain "forever wild." Forest Preserve lands may not be leased to private individuals nor may any of the timber on these lands be sold or cut. Over the years, specific amendments to the state constitution have permitted the use of Forest Preserve lands for projects such as the Adirondack Northway and the ski centers on Whiteface and Gore Mountains. Development on the rest of the Forest Preserve has been limited to primitive trails and other facilities such as lean-tos to facilitate public recreation.

In 1972 the State Land Master Plan further classified Forest Preserve lands as either "wilderness," "primitive," "wild forest," or "intensive use." For cross-country skiers, the major significance of these classifications is that snowmobile trails may exist on lands classified as "wild forest" but not in "wilderness" or "primitive" areas. Mechanical grooming of ski trails is permitted only in the "intensive use" areas at Mt. Van Hoevenberg and Gore Mt. All other cross-country ski centers in the Adirondacks are on private land.

The topographic maps accompanying all ADK hiking guides delineate private and public land, and most identify the classification of each public parcel. Descriptions in this guide will mention the classification of the land where it has any importance for the skier.

One must be aware that parts of many of these tours—particularly the trailhead areas—are on private land. This demands the utmost courtesy and respect for the landowner since many access points to public lands exist only by tradition and the continuing kindness of landowners. Park vehicles so that they cannot possibly be blocking any private access. It should go without saying that camping and the building of fires are prohibited on private land. Skiers should also be aware that there can be special restrictions on certain pieces of private land, such as no dogs allowed on the road to the Lower Ausable Lake (Trip #6).

Snowmobile Trails: On public Forest Preserve land in the Adirondacks and Catskills, snowmobiles are restricted to those trails specifically designated for snowmobiling. There are no designated snowmobile trails in areas classified "wilderness" or "primitive," but currently there are about 900 miles of designated snowmobile trail in areas classified "wild forest." Additionally, there are many more miles of established snowmobile trails on private land.

A few of the trips in this guide follow designated snowmobile trails, and the introduction to each trip gives some indication of the average level of use by snowmobilers. The snowmobile trails included in this guide do not usually receive heavy use, but on any given day one may have to share the trail with some machines. When skiing on snowmobile trails, use extra caution—especially on downhills—in the event one encounters a snowmobile. (Modern snowmobiles are much quieter than earlier models, so don't rely on a "sound" test to determine whether there are snowmobiles in the vicinity.)

When encountering snowmobiles operating on a designated trail, common courtesy should prevail regardless of one's personal feelings about such motorized recreation. If one suspects illegal snowmobile use, report the registration numbers to a forest ranger. In general, illegal use of public lands has not been a common problem. Most snowmobilers have respected those trails not open to them.

HOW TO USE THIS GUIDE

Arrangement of Trips: For each region, trips are located by number on a page map at the beginning of each section. Within each region, the most popular tours are described first and in somewhat greater detail to help familiarize skiers with the possibilities each region offers. Additional trips in each region are described in enough detail so that one can follow the route, but supplementary information on the area's history or natural features has been omitted so that more descriptions could be included in the guide.

In the heading of each description, reference is made to the corresponding volume in the ADK Forest Preserve Series of hiking guides, should a skier desire additional information. (To order, call 800-395-8080, M–F, 8:30–4:30)

Maps: Each heading also contains a list of the topographic maps available for the particular trip. In addition to the basic U.S. Geological Survey series of maps, the Adirondack Mountain Club publishes topographic maps to accompany its hiking guides; these maps are available separately from the guidebooks. Because the regions in this guide correspond to the regions of the ADK guidebook series, those maps will cover most trips within a given region. These regional maps combine several U.S. Geological sheets at a cost less than buying each sheet, while furthermore providing the most recent trail data.

Page maps have been provided for each tour. These and the text will get you to the trailhead and familiarize you with significant features of the tour, but only the text should be relied upon for exact distance figures.

The legend for the page maps follows:

LEGEND

– – – ＼	Ski Trail	③	Route Number
• • • •	Hiking Trail	▲	Mountain
P	Parking	🛖	Lean-to
＼	Barrier	⚶	Waterfall
	🌿 Swamp		

Distances: When a trip follows a hiking trail described in an ADK guide, those distances—derived from either surveyor's wheel or pedometer measurements—are used. When such measurements are not available, distances have been derived from estimates on the trail and map measurements.

Times: No attempt has been made to estimate times for any trip as differing snow conditions, the variable of breaking trail in different snow depths, and widely divergent skiing abilities make it impossible to establish a "standard" time against which a skier can reliably compare his or her own time. In general, when skiing in a broken track with powder or similarly fast snow, one should be able to travel a bit faster than a normal summer hiking pace. When breaking trail, however, one's speed can often drop below 1 mph. The best advice is to start early, know when the sun sets, watch the time carefully, and on point-to-point or loop trips be prepared to retreat along the broken track at an agreed upon time—even if more than halfway to the destination.

Difficulty Ratings: Judging one's ability as a skier is at best a difficult proposition. Ego and one's endurance as a hiker often cloud the perception of how well one can actually maneuver with a pair of skinny, slippery boards attached to one's feet. All things being equal, one should be able to ski for about as many hours as one can hike in the summer, but inexperienced skiers often end up wasting so much energy on technique that even those with generally good endurance can become quite fatigued after only a few miles. With fatigue, one's technique deteriorates further in a frustrating, if not frightening, downward spiral.

These difficulty ratings refer only to the technical difficulty of the terrain (both up and down) and not to the overall difficulty of a trip. If in doubt, start with shorter trips to determine just how much stamina one has on skis before venturing off on a 15-mile traverse.

Perhaps the best definitions of "novice," "intermediate," and "expert" come from John Frado, formerly the manager of Northfield Mountain Cross-country Center in Massachusetts. A novice, says Frado, "needs a darn good snowplow," while an intermediate "has a darn good snowplow." A true expert, by contrast, "can do a darn good snowplow while eating his lunch." A less imaginative definition is as follows:

NOVICE—A person who has skied several times and feels comfortable sliding on skis on easy terrain. Distinguished from a " beginner," who should learn on a golf course or preferably take lessons at a cross-country ski center.

INTERMEDIATE—A stronger skier who can climb moderate hills straight up and steeper hills with a herringbone, control his speed with a snowplow, and make turns on moderate terrain.

EXPERT—An experienced skier who can handle steeper terrain, including turning and stopping under a variety of snow conditions. Far beyond the category of "expert" as defined above are the cross-country downhill aficionados who can telemark through the tightest forest or look graceful even when skiing the most uneven windpack; no trips described in this guide require that degree of expertise.

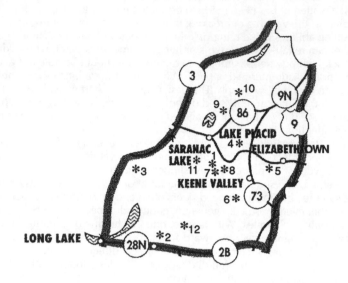

HIGH PEAKS REGION

Novice
  2. Newcomb Lake and Camp Santanoni

Novice–Intermediate
  6. Lower Ausable Lake
  9. Connery Pond to Whiteface Landing
10. Whiteface Mountain Memorial Highway

Intermediate
  3. Raquette Falls
  4. Jackrabbit Trail
  8. Mr. Van Ski Trail
11. Wanika Falls

Intermediate–Expert
  1. Marcy Dam, Avalanche Lake and Lake Colden
  5. Owl Head Lookout
12. Flowed Lands and Lake Colden from Upper Works

Expert
  7. Mt. Marcy

HIGH PEAKS REGION

The High Peaks offer some of the most spectacular cross-country ski terrain to be found anywhere in the northeast. Partly for this reason and partly because of their familiarity to summer hikers, the High Peaks are also the most popular place to ski. This does not mean, however, that the High Peaks always have the best conditions (they often don't) or that there is no comparable skiing experience elsewhere. Don't limit your skiing to this region exclusively. Nevertheless, a ski up Marcy or through Avalanche Pass is an experience no skier should miss.

The High Peaks region has a number of developed facilities at or near its periphery that cater to cross-country skiers. The closest is Adirondak Loj, which is operated by the Adirondack Mountain Club (ADK) and features a network of ski trails, a wide practice slope, and a warming building, site of ADK's High Peaks Information Center, where skiers can find rentals, a small selection of equipment, and advice on weather and trail conditions. There is a $7.00 per day parking charge—money that not only helps maintain the parking lot, but also supports ADK's broader trail maintenance and education programs. The Loj also has a weather and information phone offering current conditions on tape 24 hours a day (see list below). A source specifically for ski conditions throughout the region is the Adirondack Ski Touring Council.

Like the Adirondacks as a whole, the southern and western sides of the High Peaks receive the most snow, and it has not been uncommon to have nearly bare ground in Lake Placid and at the Loj while Newcomb has over a foot of snow and great skiing. A satellite Adirondack Park Visitor Center in Newcomb offers information on local conditions plus some limited skiing on its own trail system.

High Peaks Cross-country Ski Centers
Adirondak Loj, Lake Placid (518) 523-3518 (weather line) (518) 523-3441 (office)
Adirondack Park Visitor Center, Newcomb (518) 582-2000
Adirondack Ski Touring Council, Lake Placid (518) 523-1365
Cascade Cross-Country Ski Center, Lake Placid (518) 523-9605
Cunningham's Ski Barn, Lake Placid (518) 523-4460
Mt. Van Hoevenberg X-C Ski Center, Lake Placid (518) 523-2811
Whiteface Inn Nordic Center, Lake Placid (518) 523-2551

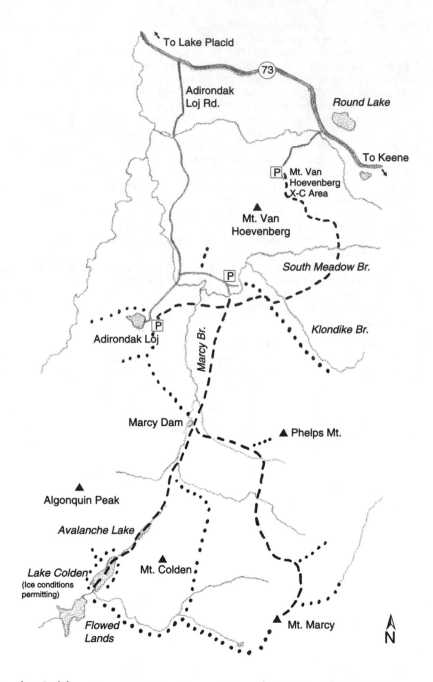

Lake Colden Tours (1), Mt. Marcy (7) and Mr. Van Ski Trail (8)

1. MARCY DAM, AVALANCHE LAKE, AND LAKE COLDEN

Distance: 12 mi., round-trip to Lake Colden
Difficulty: Intermediate–Expert
ADK Guide and Map: High Peaks
USGS Maps: Mt. Marcy 15', 1953 or Mt. Marcy and Keene Valley metric series

With spectacular scenery, easy access, and a virtual guarantee of a broken track, Lake Colden has been a popular destination for many years. (The shorter, 6-mi. round-trip to Marcy Dam on the truck trail is a very pleasant trip in its own right.) To reach Lake Colden there is 1/2 mi. of steep skiing to reach and return from the top of Avalanche Pass, but any reasonably strong skier can at least survive this pitch without too much trouble.

While hikers heading for Marcy Dam prefer the shorter approach from Adirondak Loj, skiers usually use the wide, well-graded Marcy Dam Truck Trail from South Meadows even though it is 0.6 to 1.6 mi. longer, depending on how much of the South Meadow Road is plowed. This approach is found by turning off Rt. 73 4 mi. SE of Lake Placid or approximately 11 mi. from Keene. Three and eight-tenths of a mile from Rt. 73, South Meadow Road diverges L and is marked by a small sign. The road is sometimes plowed but rarely sanded; if you have any doubt about getting back out (some of the return is uphill), park your car at the beginning of the road and ski in. At 0.9 mi. from Adirondak Loj Rd. there is some limited parking available where a usually unplowed road branches R and leads in 200 yds. to the gate at the actual start of the truck trail. (There is additional parking 1/4 mi. past this junction with an obvious trail leading through the pines to the truck trail gate.)

From the register at the gate (0 mi.) the trail is flat for 0.3 mi. to a junction with the Mr. Van Ski Trail (see map) after which the trail climbs in a series of mostly gentle rolls to Marcy Dam at 2.8 mi. The interior outpost here is not staffed in winter but there are seven lean-tos (as of 1992) around the pond. Continuing from the dam and register, one briefly follows the blue-marked trail to Marcy before turning R and following yellow markers for the gentle climb to Avalanche Camps at 3.9 mi. The next half-mile is often called "Misery Hill," but a skier's bypass takes away at least some of the "misery" on the ascent and considerably mitigates the "terror" on the way down. (Skiers who don't feel capable of skiing this section can, if it is packed firm enough, remove their skis and walk up or down the hiking trail. DON'T WALK ON THE SKI TRAIL as "post holes" are practically inevitable and quite dangerous to any skier.)

From Avalanche Camps, the skier's bypass is found by starting L and up the blue-marked trail to Lake Arnold for about 200 yds. and then continuing straight ahead where the Lake Arnold Trail turns sharp L. The ski trail climbs moderately to steeply to a crossing of the hiking trail about 0.3 mi. from Avalanche Camps. Continuing across the hiking trail, the ski trail switchbacks L and recrosses the hiking trail in 300 yds. This is followed by a switchback to the R to rejoin the hiking trail on the flat just before reaching the top of Avalanche Pass at 4.4 mi.

Once over the pass, the trail narrows and twists between boulders and under ice-covered cliffs before descending in a few short pitches to Avalanche Lake at 5 mi. The spectacular cliffs rising up on both sides make a natural wind tunnel, so be prepared to don a windproof layer and perhaps goggles and face mask for the 0.5-mi. ski across the lake. Entering the woods at 5.5 mi., the trail descends to a junction and register at 5.8 mi.,where the hiking trail splits to go along the E and W shores of Lake Colden. The easiest skiing, however, is found by continuing straight ahead and following the old phone line (marked with an occasional yellow DEC ski trail disk) to the N end of Lake Colden at 6 mi.

The DEC's Interior Outpost (usually staffed in winter) is located midway down the W shore, and two lean-tos with spectacular views on the far shore offer a good place to rest and eat lunch. To continue on to Flowed Lands, ski past the dam at the S end of Lake Colden, cross the Opalescent River, and ski along a trail on the L bank about 1/3 mi. to the N end of the open area (which was flooded until 1979). If continuing on through to Upper Works, head SW across the open area to find the trail at Calamity Lean-to. **ADK**

Algonquin from Mt. Jo

Carl Heilman

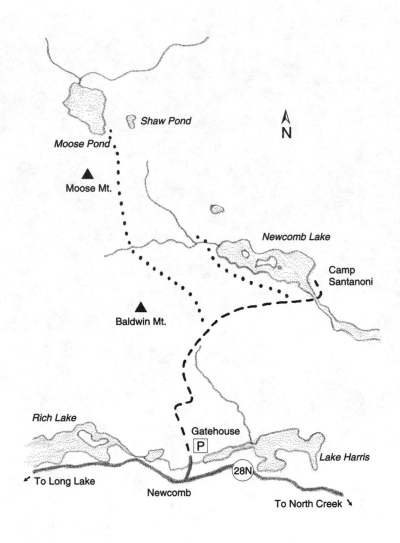

Newcomb Lake and Camp Santanoni (2)

2. NEWCOMB LAKE
AND CAMP SANTANONI

Distance: 9.4 mi., round-trip
Difficulty: Novice
ADK Guide and Map: High Peaks
USGS Maps: Santanoni and Newcomb 15′, 1953 or Santanoni Peak and Newcomb
metric series

Offering gentle grades, a smooth road, and a beautiful destination, this has been a
popular trip ever since the state acquired this parcel of land in 1973. And in some
of the recent snow drought years, the Newcomb area has often been the only place
in the entire northeast where there was any good cross-country skiing to be had. In
addition to the trip described below, there are many other longer trips possible,
including a 13.5-mi. round-trip to Moose Pond and several overnight trip possibilities on the horse trail system along the Cold River and on to Coreys or Lake Placid.

The access to Newcomb Lake is found at the west end of the village of
Newcomb (0.3 mi. W of Newcomb Town Hall) and is marked with a sign for the
Santanoni Preserve. A narrow road leads 0.3 mi. across a bridge and up past the
gate house, where there is parking to the R. From the gate and register (0 mi.) the
road is flat for 0.9 mi. to some old farm buildings, after which a short climb leads to
a view of the Santanoni Range at 1.1 mi. A gentle descent and climb brings the
road to a junction at 2.2 mi. (Road L leads 4.5 mi. to Moose Pond.) Continuing to
climb gently, the road levels off and begins to descend gently at 3.2 mi., passing a
junction with the hiking trail along the S side of Newcomb Lake at 3.7 mi. The road
continues its gentle descent and crosses Newcomb Lake on a bridge at 4.4 mi.
before swinging L along the N shore to Camp Santanoni at 4.7 mi.

While the actual skiing required to reach this classic Adirondack "great camp"
is simple and straightforward, this property and camp have both a long history and
a present situation that is anything but simple and straightforward.

Completed in 1893 by Robert C. Pruyn of Albany, Camp Santanoni was the
centerpiece of his 12,000 acre Santanoni Preserve. The camp was designed by
Robert H. Robertson, then a prominent New York City architect. In 1903 Delano
and Aldrich, another New York architectural firm, designed the farm complex with
William Delano himself designing the gatehouse which was built in 1905. Robert
Pruyn continued to enjoy his property until his death in 1934. In 1950, Pruyn's
estate offered the entire property to the State for $145,000. No funds were then
available so in 1953 the property was bought by the Melvin family.

The Melvin family also made several offers to sell the property to the
State, but it was not until 1972 that the Nature Conservancy facilitated the transfer.
Initially, all buildings were to be torn down as that was and is the DEC's policy. An
understandable reluctance to destroy such a large and unique structure led to an
exception being made in the case of structures listed on the State Register of
Historic Places. Thus Camp Santanoni and the other buildings still stand, and
preservation work has begun on some of the most critically deteriorated structures.
The exact use for this complex has yet to be determined, but no change is
anticipated in the ability of skiers to continue to ski the road to visit this unique
piece of Adirondack history. **ADK**

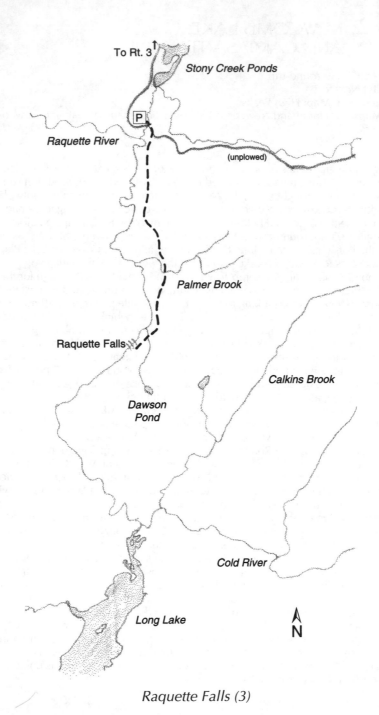

To Rt. 3

Stony Creek Ponds

P

Raquette River

(unplowed)

Palmer Brook

Raquette Falls

Calkins Brook

Dawson
Pond

Cold River

Long Lake

N

Raquette Falls (3)

3. RAQUETTE FALLS

Distance: 9 mi., round-trip
Difficulty: Intermediate
ADK Guide and Map: High Peaks
USGS Maps: Long Lake 15' or Tupper Lake metric series

This justly popular trip reaches a spectacular destination with relatively little effort and only a few short stretches of difficult skiing. This area often has better snow conditions than areas closer to the High Peaks, and this tour's popularity means there will usually be a good broken track within a day or so of any storm. The start of this trip is also the starting point for longer trips to Duck Hole, Shattuck Clearing, and Newcomb.

The start is at the end of Coreys Rd off Rt. 3, 12.7 mi. W of the traffic light in the center of Saranac Lake Village and 2.7 mi. E of the junction of Rtes. 3 and 30 east of Tupper Lake. The road is marked with a large DEC sign reading "High Peaks via Duck Hole." Coreys Rd. is plowed for 2.5 mi. to the bridge over Stony Creek. There is usually a good parking area plowed here, but park carefully as this is also where the plow turns around. Do not block the bridge.

Starting at the bridge (0 mi.), the route follows the road for 0.3 mi. to a small parking area on the R with a trail register box. Turning R and passing the register, the trail begins climbing gently. At 2.0 mi. the trail crosses a small brook and climbs more steeply for 100 yds. before coming to a junction with a side trail to Hemlock Hill Lean-to at 2.4 mi. The trail then dips down to a junction at Palmer Brook at 2.5 mi. (The trail going straight leads to Calkins Brook at 7.0 mi. and Shattuck Clearing at 11.5 mi.)

Turning R, the trail to Raquette Falls crosses Palmer Brook and begins to climb. (Those using the metric series map will be relieved to know that the route does not go over the top of the hill as shown, but skirts to the north and east.) After descending to the edge of a slough of the Raquette River at 3.1 mi., the trail has several small ups and downs before beginning a longer climb to a crest at 4.1 mi. The trail now descends via a series of steep switchbacks that will challenge one's proficiency at snowplowing before reaching the signpost at the canoe carry at 4.5 mi. The DEC Interior Outpost (not staffed in winter) is up and to the L. To reach the actual falls, continue up the canoe carry approximately 100 yds. and then turn R on a vague trail leading approximately 0.3 mi. to a falls at the head of a gorge. With good snow cover, one can continue along this trail to see the entire 1-mi. section of rapids, with the canoe carry making a good return route. Another worthwhile side trip is Dawson Pond, reached by a 0.7-mi. trail that is found at the SE corner of the large field S of the Interior Outpost. **ADK**

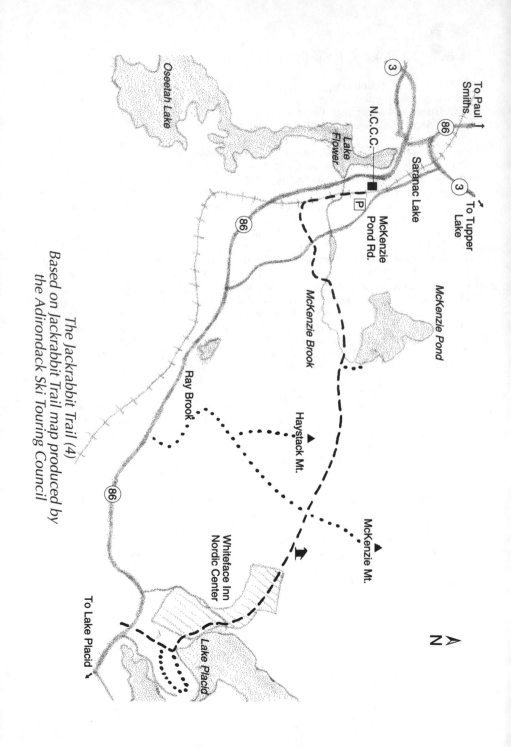

The Jackrabbit Trail (4)
Based on Jackrabbit Trail map produced by
the Adirondack Ski Touring Council

16

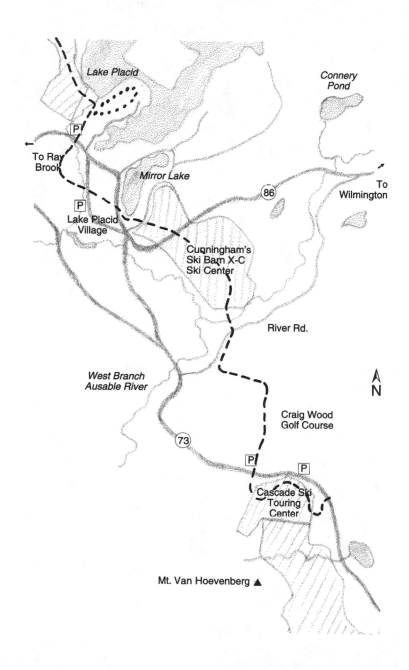

The Jackrabbit Trail (4) (cont)

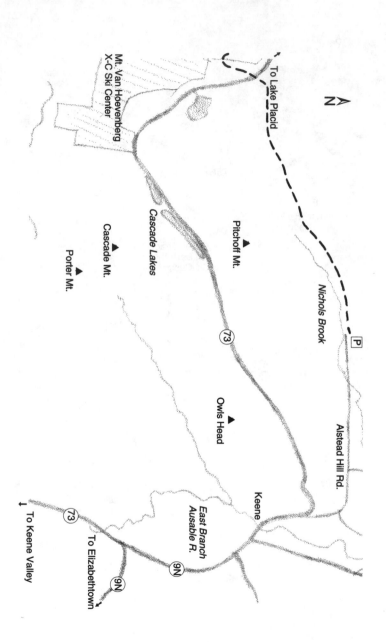

The Jackrabbit Trail (4) (cont)

4. THE JACKRABBIT TRAIL

Distance: 24 mi., Saranac Lake to Keene (some distances estimated)
Difficulty: Intermediate
ADK Guide and Map: High Peaks (but not every trail section described)
USGS Maps: Lake Placid, Mt. Marcy, Saranac Lake 15' or Lake Placid, Keene Valley, and Saranac Lake metric series

Started in 1986, the Jackrabbit Trail is a unique opportunity for cross-country skiing. It links populated areas, developed cross-country ski centers, and some longer sections of wilderness skiing to make possible a tremendous variety of ski trips. The construction and maintenance of the Jackrabbit Trail is the major project of the Adirondack Ski Touring Council (ASTC), a membership organization composed of local businesses and interested skiers. Since its inception, ASTC has forged a partnership of skiers, businesses and landowners that first stitched together this continuous route and has since then funded continuing improvements on the trail. Much of the trail on private land is groomed by the adjacent ski centers, and a trail fee is required on most groomed sections. As of 1996, one ticket is good at all area ski centers. Check the latest Jackrabbit Trail map for current information.

The trail is named in honor of Herman "Jack Rabbit" Johannsen, who was a legendary skiing pioneer both in the Adirondacks and, later, in Canada. There he constructed the famous Maple Leaf Trail and helped to start the 100-mile, two-day Canadian Ski Marathon. While living and vacationing in Lake Placid between 1916 and 1928, Johannsen laid out some of the original routes used by today's trail. He was also famous for his one-day ascents of Marcy starting from Lake Placid—a round-trip of over 30 miles. "Jack Rabbit" died in 1987 in his native Norway at age 111, skiing nearly to the time of his death.

Future plans include expansion of the Jackrabbit Trail to Tupper Lake and the Visitor's Interpretive Center in Paul Smiths. ASTC publishes an annual map of the Jackrabbit Trail, available free of charge at local ski shops and other businesses or by mail (with self-addressed envelope and postage for 2 oz.) from: ASTC, P.O. Box 843, Lake Placid NY 12946. The map contains information on membership in the Council; all skiers should consider supporting this organization. ASTC also provides cross-country ski conditions by phone (518-523-1365).

One can start skiing from many points on the trail and ski as much or as little of the trail as one desires, so the following brief description from Saranac Lake to Keene is not the only way to "do" the trail. The entire trail is marked with large red rectangular markers bearing the logo of the Adirondack Ski Touring Council and the Jackrabbit Trail. Distance is given for each major section with cumulative totals in parentheses.

SARANAC LAKE TO MCKENZIE POND ROAD—1.5 mi.

Starting in Saranac Lake, one can ski from the town hall via Riverside Park, but the best access point is at the North Country Community College gymnasium, which is found by following the signs from Rt. 86 in Saranac Lake. From the gymnasium, parking lot (0 mi.), the trail follows the abandoned railroad tracks for 0.5 mi. and then turns sharp L and up through a pine grove to join an old snowmobile trail at 0.7 mi. Turning L, the Jackrabbit Trail follows the snowmobile trail for another 0.8 mi. before turning R to McKenzie Pond Rd. at 1.5 mi. The Jackrabbit Trail resumes on the other side of the road, 100 yds. to the R (east). McKenzie Pond Rd. is the beginning of a 5.5-mi. wilderness section and is a popular start/finish point.

MCKENZIE POND ROAD TO WHITEFACE INN—5.5 mi.

From McKenzie Pond Rd.(0 mi.) the trail climbs to a clearing next to a softball field and then bears L and enters the woods for a short descent to a power line. Swinging R on the power line, the trail soon leaves the power line by bearing L and reaches state land at 0.5 mi. This is the beginning of a 0.6 mi. section of new (1995) trail that joins the old truck trail at 1.1 mi. and reaches McKenzie Pond at 1.9 mi.

From here it is a 1.5 mi. continuous climb to a pass between Haystack and McKenzie Mts. Skied in this direction, it is merely a long climb; but skied in the other direction it requires a bit more than intermediate skill to negotiate. (Those who can negotiate this hill, however, consider it one of the finest runs in the Adirondacks available to cross-country skiers.) After cresting the pass, the trail descends moderately to a four-way junction at 4 mi. (Red trail R leads to Rt. 86; red trail L leads to the summit of McKenzie Mt.) Continuing straight ahead on the near flat, the trail passes a lean-to on the L at 4.5 mi. and begins a gradual descent for 0.7 mi. to the upper edge of the Whiteface Inn Nordic Center. From here the descent steepens for the final 0.8 m i. to the Whiteface Inn Road at 6 mi. (7.5 mi. from North Country Community College).

WHITEFACE INN TO MIRROR LAKE—3.5 mi.

The character of the next section of the trail is radically different, as it winds its way around and through the Village of Lake Placid. There are a number of road crossings and just over 0.3 mi. of road walking. To continue, turn R just before reaching Whiteface Inn Rd. and ski 200 yds. to a gate and road crossing opposite the Whiteface Inn golf course. After crossing the road (0 mi.), bear slightly left to arrive at the golf house, which serves as the headquarters for the nordic center. (As of 1996 there was a $10.00-a-day trail fee, but new ownership may change this and/or the current policy of letting skiers pass through without charge.) Passing to the left of the golf house, the trail crosses a bridge and an access road and then heads along the L edge of a fairway to the top of a hill. Here the Jackrabbit Trail turns sharp L and enters the woods for 50 yds. before emerging at the top of a steep descent on another fairway. Bearing L at the bottom of this hill, the trail joins a woods road paralleling the fairway for 150 yds. before swinging sharp L to reach a bridge below the Lake Placid dam at 0.8 mi.

Crossing the bridge, the trail swings sharp R and proceeds on the flat for 0.3 mi. to another sharp R across a small bridge, and then presents some minor ups and downs to the parking lot at the Howard Johnson's Restaurant on Saranac Ave. at 1.7 mi. Now crossing Saranac Ave., most skiers will end up walking for 200 yds. to the left of a Sugar Creek store and down the road past the Lake Placid Center for the Arts to a bridge across the Lake Placid Outlet (Cold Brook). Past the bridge, the trail resumes on the R, climbs into the woods, and then swings L to cross the road at 2.2 mi., after which it descends through thick woods to a ski bridge over the Lake Placid Outlet. After a few more ups and downs, the trail reaches West Valley Rd., crosses it, and climbs moderately to the Holiday Inn at the top of a hill at 3.2 mi. To continue, walk past the Holiday Inn and descend to the Lake Placid Post Office. Bearing L of the Post Office, cross under the Lake Placid Toboggan Slide to the S end of Mirror Lake at 3.5 mi. (11 mi. from N.C.C.C . in Saranac Lake). When snow and ice conditions permit, ASTC grooms and sets track on the lake to provide "downtown" skiing plus access to the numerous lodges and restaurants on or near the lake.

MIRROR LAKE TO CASCADE CROSS-COUNTRY SKI CENTER—6.5 mi.

From the S end of Mirror Lake (0 mi.), the trail crosses Mirror Lake Dr. and heads to the R of a large building that was once the employee dormitory of the Lake Placid Club. It then passes to the R of three abandoned cottages, goes up a small hill, and bears L past an unfinished condominium complex to the golf house that houses Cunningham's cross-country center. (The Lake Placid Club property was sold in 1996, and the new owner's plans may cause any or all of the landmarks mentioned here—including Cunningham's Ski Barn—to change in the next few years.)

From the golf house, the Jackrabbit Trail follows the ski center trails down across Rt. 86, onto the lower golf course to a point 2.5 mi. from Mirror Lake. Leaving Cunningham's system, the trail descends gradually 150 yds. to an open field, swings sharp L, and comes to a gate in another 100 yds. Passing the gate, the trail soon starts down through a field and around a house to a vehicular bridge across the W. Branch of the Ausable River at 3 mi.

Crossing the bridge and River Rd., the trail parallels the road for 0.2 mi. and then rejoins the road briefly before turning sharp L and up a side road leading to a private driveway (plowed but not usually sanded for 150 yds.). Consistent skiing begins again at 3.5 mi. The trail now follows an unplowed road for 0.2 mi., bears R on another road, and then goes L through a gate before beginning a moderate climb to Craig Wood Golf Course. Crossing the golf course pretty much from N to S, the trail reenters the woods just to the L of a small maintenance shop and climbs gently to Rt. 73 at 5 mi. Crossing Rt. 73, the Jackrabbit Trail enters the outskirts of the Cascade Cross-Country Ski Center's trails and goes through the woods for nearly 0.3 mi. of flat skiing, after which the trail descends along an unplowed road before turning sharp L into thick woods. Descent continues for another 0.2 mi. Then a short steep climb leads to a junction with the main part of the Cascade system. Turning sharp L, the Jackrabbit Trail climbs gently for 0.7 mi. to the lodge at 6.5 mi. (18 mi. from N.C.C.C. in Saranac Lake). As of 1996, Cascade grooms the trail from River Road to the lodge—trail fee required. Skiers may, however, come in to the lodge from Keene without charge. Those who wish to start at Cascade should check in at the ski shop and expect to pay a nominal parking fee.

CASCADE CROSS-COUNTRY SKI CENTER TO KEENE—6 mi.

Past the lodge (0 mi.), the marked route of the Jackrabbit Trail follows the "Beaver Run" trail, but as this 0.8-mi. section is quite rough it may be closed even though the rest of the trail is skiable. In this case, ask at the ski shop for the best route to continue. With good snow Beaver Run is a delightful, gentle downhill run to a semi-open swamp, after which the Jackrabbit Trail exits the Cascade system by turning sharp L at the top of a small hill. (Trail straight ahead leads to Mt. Van Hoevenberg X-C Ski Center—separate trail fee required.)

Now following a wider trail, the Jackrabbit Trail dips down and up across a small brook, swings sharp L, and continues mostly on the level to Rt. 73, which is crossed at 1.5 mi. (This has long been a popular starting point for those wishing simply to enjoy the mostly downhill 4.5-mi. run to Keene. On a busy weekend, however, parking can be a problem here, and skiers are encouraged to start at Cascade Cross-Country Ski Center [0.5 mi. W by road]. Cascade asks a nominal parking fee but offers a ski shop, restaurant, and restrooms plus an extra 1.5 mi. of skiing.)

After crossing Rt. 73, the Jackrabbit Trail follows a road that is usually plowed but not sanded for 0.5 mi. to the top of a hill, after which the plowing ends. From here, there are gentle ups and downs to a large beaver pond at 3.3 mi. with a spectacular view of Pitchoff's ice-covered cliffs. After a short climb, the trail crests the pass at 3.2 mi. and begins a moderate descent. Caution is advised on this first part as the grade is steady for 0.2 mi. to a bridge, below which there is a steep, sometimes rough, pitch before the trail levels out on a lower beaver pond. Continuing to descend at a gentle grade past this pond, the trail crosses two more small bridges and descends moderately to another old beaver pond at 5 mi. After another 0.2 mi. of moderate descent, the trail flattens as it approaches the Keene end of the trail at 6 mi. (24 mi. from Saranac Lake).

This trailhead is reached by road by turning off Rt. 73 onto Alstead Hill Rd. (County Road 40) 0.9 mi. up from Keene. Follow Alstead Hill Rd. past the Bark Eater Inn and to its end 3.9 mi. from Keene. Here there is a small parking lot and Adirondack Rock and River, an inn and guide service. **ADK**

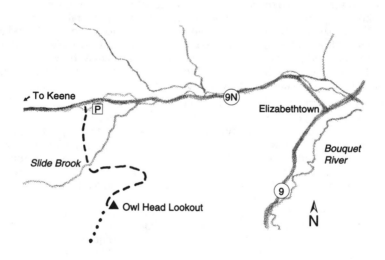

Owl Head Lookout (5)

5. OWL HEAD LOOKOUT

Distance: 5.4 mi., round-trip
Difficulty: Intermediate–Expert
ADK Guide and Map: High Peaks
USGS Maps: Elizabethtown 15' or Elizabethtown metric series

Ski tours to spectacular summits are rare, but this trip is one of the easiest by which to reach such a remarkable view. Skiing this route requires 1-1/2 to 2 feet of snow, but it is well worth waiting for the right conditions to do this trip.

The start is on Rt. 9N, 4.5 mi. from Rt. 9 in Elizabethtown and 5.5 mi. from the junction of Rtes. 9N and 73 between Keene and Keene Valley. It is marked by a large DEC sign. The trail is marked with red disks. From the highway (0 mi.) the trail follows a road a few yards down to a bridge and then diverges L and begins a gentle climb. Crossing Slide Brook at 1.1 mi., the trail begins to climb more steeply, levels out at 1.8, swings R, and then climbs in moderate stages to a junction at the crest of a ridge at 2.5 mi. Owl Head Lookout is up and to the L. One may ski a few yards up the trail before resorting to walking for the final few yards to the open rock, which offers spectacular views of Giant and Rocky Peak with Lake Champlain and numerous other peaks visible. **ADK**

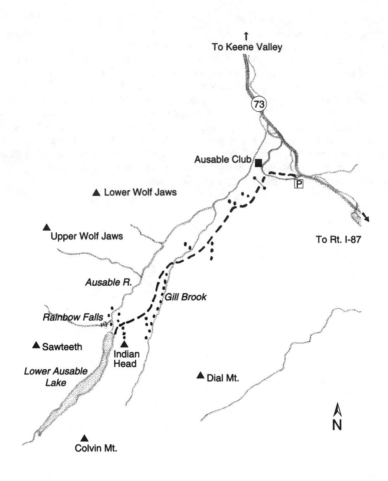

Lower Ausable Lake (6)

6. LOWER AUSABLE LAKE

Distance: 8.2 mi., round-trip
Difficulty: Novice–Intermediate
ADK Guide and Map: High Peaks
USGS Maps: Mt. Marcy 15' or Keene Valley and Mt. Marcy metric series

A ski up the graded gravel road to the Lower Ausable Lake has long been a popular ski—especially for early season or low snow conditions. When conditions are right, the ski up is delightful, the scenery spectacular, and the return—in about half the ascent time—pure joy. Mitigating these pluses, however, are that one must park 0.5 mi. from the start of actual skiing (although this distance can sometimes be skied), that vehicular traffic on the road may make surface conditions less than ideal, and that dogs are not permitted under any conditions. The entire trip is on private land, courtesy of a public easement granted by the Adirondack Mountain Reserve. This area has been managed for over a century as a game preserve. Hunting is prohibited, with the ban on dogs to further protect the game; because of these restrictions one is far more likely to see deer here than on any other trip.

The public parking area is just off Rt. 73 on a side road 3.3 mi. S of Keene Valley and 5.6 mi. N of the junction of Rtes. 9 and 73 near Exit 30. From the parking area (0 mi.) head W along the road and eventually along the edge of a golf course for 0.6 mi. Just before the main building, turn L and down a road between two tennis courts for 300 yds. to a register and small watchman's hut. Continue straight ahead from the register to an elaborate wooden gate at the actual start of the Lake Road. Landmarks along the road include a crossing of Gill Brook (followed by a moderate climb) at 1.9 mi., a small reservoir on the L at 2.5 mi., and the Lower Lake at 4.1 mi. Due to frequent strong winds, ice conditions on the lake are usually unfavorable for skiing; but with good snow, an interesting side trip of 0.5 mi. round-trip is possible to Rainbow Falls, which is reached by crossing the bridge just below the Lower Lake dam and following the signs to the base of the falls. **ADK**

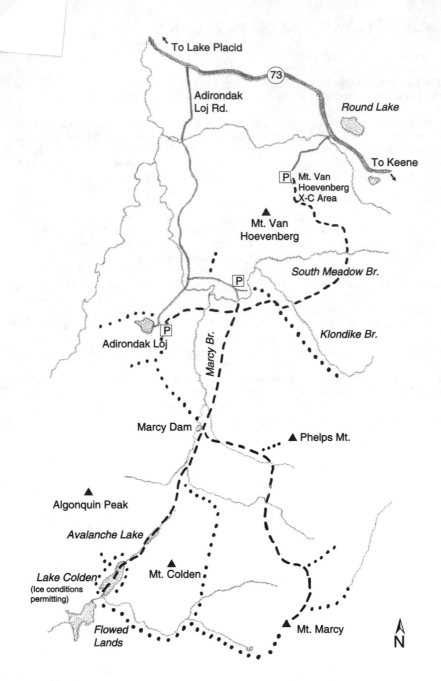

Mt. Marcy (7), Lake Colden Tours (1) and Mr. Van Ski Trail (8)

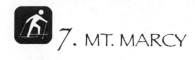

7. MT. MARCY

Distance: 16 mi., round-trip
Difficulty: Expert
ADK Guide and Map: High Peaks
USGS Maps: Mt. Marcy 15' or Keene Valley and Mt. Marcy metric series

Though not for everyone, a ski ascent of Marcy remains one of the Adirondacks' greatest trips. On a warm day with good conditions, the trip can appear deceptively easy; but under no circumstances should the trip be underestimated. Conditions above treeline can be vastly different from those experienced up to the Plateau at 4,600 ft.; beyond this point crampons, face mask, and ice axe may be necessary to actually reach the summit. Should clouds close in, a compass and the unquestioned ability to use it are required to return safely to one's ascent route and not end up straying into the decidedly unfriendly terrain of Panther Gorge.

The start is the same as for Lake Colden. At Marcy Dam at 2.8 mi. bear L to follow the blue-marked trail to Marcy. Climbing is moderate to a bridge at 4.1 mi. after which the grade steepens. At 200 yds. above this bridge, continue straight to follow the ski route to Indian Falls, which is reached at 5.1 mi. After Indian Falls the grade moderates until it steepens briefly at 5.9 mi.; it soon moderates again as the trail works its way up to the crest of the ridge leading to a junction with the yellow-marked Hopkins Trail to Keene Valley at 6.8 mi. The former site of Plateau Lean-to at 4,600 ft. is reached at 7.1 mi.

Above here the trail narrows and steepens before reaching the junction with the Phelps Trail from Keene Valley at 7.5 mi.; in a good snow year, the signs at this junction may be totally buried. Conditions on the final 0.5 mi. to the summit vary so widely that no definitive description is possible. In general, by bearing to the L of the hiking trail route after reaching timberline one can stay on good snow practically to the summit. Do not count on being able to use the summer markings (paint and cairns) to reach and return from the summit, and definitely be prepared to turn back if there is any question about conditions. **ADK**

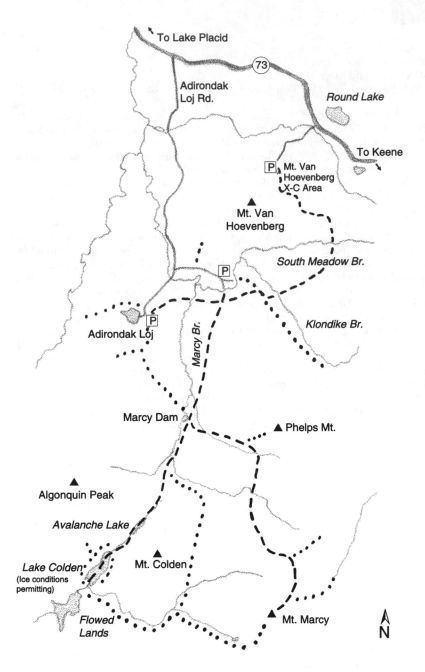

Mt. Van Ski Trail (8), Mt. Marcy (7) and Lake Colden Tours (1)

8. MR. VAN SKI TRAIL

Distance: 6.0 mi., point-to-point
Difficulty: Intermediate
ADK Guide and Map: High Peaks
USGS Maps: Mt. Marcy, 15' or Keene Valley metric series

Linking Adirondak Loj and the Mt. Van Hoevenberg X-C Center, this interesting trail can become part of many trips in the area. It is best skied from the Adirondak Loj end to Mt. Van Hoevenberg. The downhills are easier in that direction, and finding one's way up through the maze of trails at Mt. Van Hoevenberg is somewhat difficult if starting from that end. In recent years, the major problem with skiing the Mr. Van Trail has been the lack of a bridge over either Marcy Brook or South Meadow Brook. Most of the time when the conditions are good, one can cross these brooks without the bridges, but check at the Adirondak Loj for a current report.

The start is at Adirondak Loj (see introduction). Begin at the register for the trail to Marcy (0 mi.). The trip follows this trail for 200 yds., then turns sharp L at a fourway junction to follow red DEC markers gradually down to a bridge across Marcy Brook at 0.8 mi. The trail then traverses a partially open swamp, crosses the South Meadow Truck Trail at 1.3 mi., and continues with short ups and downs to the Klondike Trail at 1.9 mi. Turning R, the Mr. Van Trail follows the Klondike Trail for 250 yds. before turning L and reaching the Mr. Van Lean-to at 3.6 mi. Crossing South Meadow Brook on a bridge, the trail climbs steadily to Hi-Notch and the junction with the Mt. Van Hoevenberg system at 4.7 mi. Bearing L and down, the trail takes a sharp L, drops through one junction, and comes to a second junction with the "Ladies Olympic 5km" at 5.3 mi. Now following the "Ladies Olympic 5km" signs, the route descends, climbs two short hills, and ends with a series of sweeping turns down to the cross-country stadium at 6 mi. To date there has been no problem in following this route and simply exiting to the parking lot without paying a trail fee, but anyone staying to ski other trails in the complex must pay the daily trail fee. **ADK**

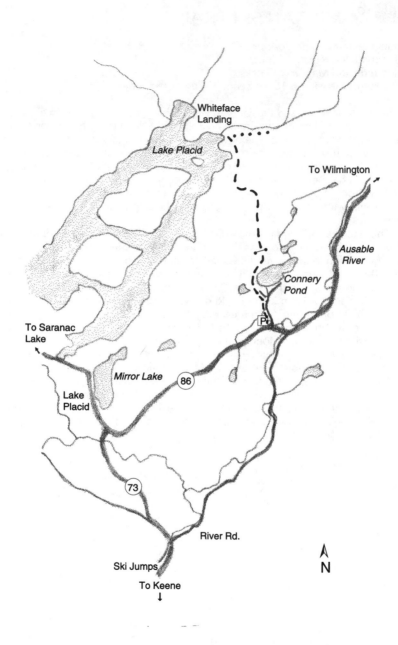

Connery Pond to Whiteface Landing (9)

9. CONNERY POND TO WHITEFACE LANDING

Distance: 6 mi., round-trip
Difficulty: Novice-Intermediate
ADK Guide and Map: High Peaks
USGS Maps: Lake Placid 15' or Lake Placid metric series

This is a justly popular trip to a scenic destination. The skiing has enough ups and downs to keep experienced skiers from being totally bored while not terrifying less experienced skiers. The start is on Rt. 86, 3.1 mi. E of the stoplight at the junction of Rtes. 73 and 86, and is marked with a DEC sign. Park cars on the highway or at a small parking area, sometimes plowed, just off the road. The trail follows a private driveway that is sometimes plowed but in any case should be skied and not driven.

From the highway (0 mi.) follow the driveway, marked with red DEC disks. At 0.2 mi. continue straight at a jct. At 0.5 mi. the marked route bears L and down, arriving in about 200 yds. past this turn at a new fisherman's access trail leading R to the pond. One can either take this trail and then ski to the NW corner of the pond, or continue on the red-marked trail past a private residence and around the W end of Connery Pond to a gate at the beginning of the truck trail at 0.9 mi. After some flat skiing the trail climbs gradually to a height of land at 1.9 mi. after which it gently descends to a junction at 3.0 mi. Whiteface Landing a t the N end of Lake Placid is a few yards to the L. **ADK**

Tony Goodwin

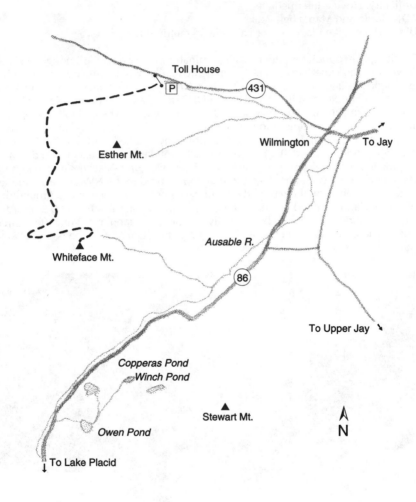

Toll House

P

431

Esther Mt.

Wilmington

To Jay

Ausable R.

86

To Upper Jay

Whiteface Mt.

Copperas Pond

Winch Pond

Stewart Mt.

N

Owen Pond

To Lake Placid

Whiteface Mountain Memorial Highway (10)

10. WHITEFACE MOUNTAIN MEMORIAL HIGHWAY

Distance: 11 mi., round-trip
Difficulty: Novice–Intermediate
ADK Guide and Map: High Peaks
USGS Maps: Lake Placid 15' or Lake Placid and Wilmington metric series

On a fair day with good snow conditions, a ski up and down Whiteface can seem like a deceptively easy way to "bag" a 4,000 ft. winter ascent. Under less than ideal conditions, however, the skiing can be treacherous and the weather just as severe as it can be on any of the peaks above timberline. Because of its high altitude and smooth surface, the highway has long been a popular early-season tour or a last resort in low snow years. After most storms a track should be quickly broken out either by other skiers or by vehicles used by researchers at the Atmospheric Sciences Research Center located just below the toll house. After a thaw and freeze cycle, however, this vehicular traffic can leave an icy, rutted, chattery mess to ski on. Remember also that the wind can blow all the snow off, exposing the pavement on corners especially. All these grim warnings aside, on more days than not the snow is just fine for this exceptionally scenic trip.

The start is at the toll house approximately 3 mi. above the village of Wilmington on Rt. 431. The "no trespassing" signs warn people not to enter any of the buildings while also serving as a reminder that the highway is officially closed in winter. From the toll house (0 mi.) the first views are at 0.8 mi., followed by a small shed on the L at 1.7 mi. At 3.2 mi. the highway crosses the base of a slide and then comes to the first hairpin turn, Lake Placid Turn, at 3.5 mi. With a view of Lake Placid (surprise!) and the steep ridge above leading to the Castle and summit, this makes a good destination if the weather is too inclement to continue. Wilmington Turn is reached at 4.5 mi., and from here conditions can range from deep drifts to glare ice to the Castle at 5.3 mi. From the Castle a summer walkway with railings leads to the summit at 5.5 mi. **ADK**

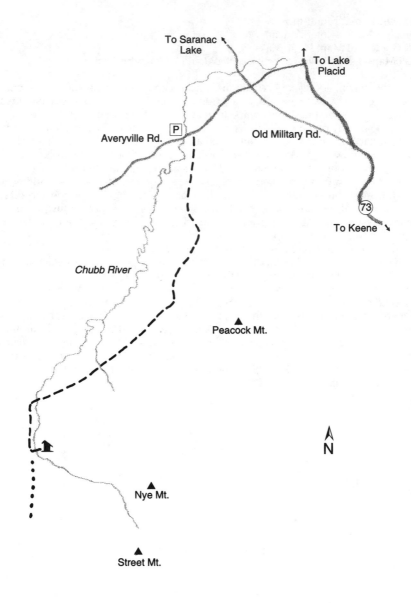

To Saranac
Lake

To Lake
Placid

Averyville Rd. P

Old Military Rd.

73

To Keene

Chubb River

Peacock Mt.

N

Nye Mt.

Street Mt.

Wanika Falls (11)
Based on ADK High Peaks map

11. WANIKA FALLS

Distance: 14 mi., round-trip
Difficulty: Intermediate
ADK Guide and Map: High Peaks
USGS Maps: Saranac Lake and Santanoni 15' or Saranac Lake and Ampersand Lake metric series

Skied far less frequently than most other High Peaks trips, this route offers some nice skiing along the way to a seldom visited series of waterfalls. The start is on Averyville Rd. south of Lake Placid at the northern terminus of the 132-mile Northville-Placid Trail. Averyville Rd. is most easily accessed from Old Military Rd., which is the bypass south of Lake Placid. From the large DEC sign for the N-P Trail at the junction of Old Military Rd. and Averyville Rd., follow Averyville Rd. 1.2 mi. S to a sign on the L. There is limited parking here, but 200 yds. beyond on the R there is additional parking.

From the road (0 mi.) the trail with blue DEC markers begins with a gradual climb of 0.5 mi. followed by rolling terrain through a variety of forest types to a beaver pond at 4.1 mi. From here one can see the new slide on the W side of Nye Mt. that came down in the earthquake of October 1983. Flatter going through open hardwoods leads to the bridge over the Chubb River at 6.1 mi. Turning L after the bridge, the trail climbs to a junction with a side trail to Wanika Falls Lean-to at 6.7 mi. The lower falls is just below this junction. The upper falls is about 100 yds. above the lean-to. **ADK**

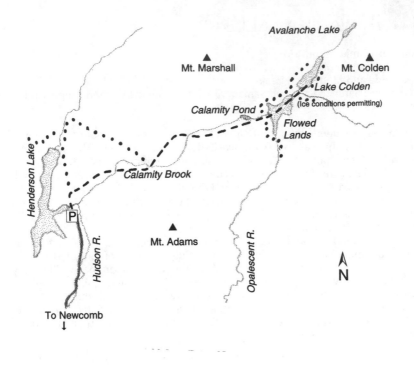

Flowed Lands and Lake Colden from Upper Works (12)

12. FLOWED LANDS AND LAKE COLDEN FROM UPPER WORKS

Distance: 9.4 mi., round-trip to Flowed Lands; 11.2 mi., round-trip to Lake Colden
Difficulty: Intermediate-Expert
ADK Map and Guidebook: High Peaks
USGS Maps: Mt. Marcy and Santanoni 15' or Mt. Marcy and Santanoni Peak metric series

The spectacular view from Flowed Lands of Mt. Colden and the MacIntyre Range combined with interesting (but not too interesting) skiing make this tour a favorite of many skiers. When done as a point-to-point traverse with the Lake Colden trip, this is one of the classic ski tours in North America. (Note: The skiing back down to Upper Works from Flowed Lands and Lake Colden is overall a bit more difficult than the skiing down Avalanche Pass on that approach to Lake Colden. On a ski-through trip, leaders may want to have those with lesser downhill skiing ability start at this end.)

The start to the Flowed Lands trip is at the end of a long, lonely road running from Rt. 28N near Newcomb past the nearly abandoned titanium mine at Tahawus to a collection of abandoned 19th-century buildings known variously as the "village of Adirondac" or "Upper Works." This road leaves Rt. 28N 7.3 mi. NW of Aiden Lair or about 5 mi. E of the Town Hall in Newcomb. At 1.6 mi. from Rt. 28N bear L, and bear L again at 6 mi. onto a narrower road marked with a sign for "Mt. Marcy and the High Peaks". Upper Works is 9.5 mi. from Rt. 28N. An alternate approach is via Blue Ridge Rd. (County Rt. 2) from North Hudson at Exit 29 on the Adirondack Northway. Drive approximately 20 mi. W from Exit 29 and turn R on the road to Tahawus. (This intersection is 1.6 mi. N of Rt. 28N.)

From the register at Upper Works (0 mi.) the red and yellow-marked trail proceeds nearly on the level to a junction at 0.4 mi. (The yellow-marked trail straight ahead leads to Indian Pass and Duck Hole.) Turning R and now following red markers, one skis along with moderate ups and downs to Calamity Brook at 1.3 mi. There is a narrow suspension bridge just downstream, but under most conditions one can cross the brook on the ice. (If one does have to use the bridge, use caution. The approach to the bridge is clearly not designed with ski use in mind.)

After crossing Calamity Brook, the trail proceeds mostly on the flat— except for one short climb and sharp descent—to a second bridge across Calamity Brook at 1.8 mi. Across the bridge is a junction with the trail from the Indian Pass Trail. This is the end of the red markers. Turning R and now following blue markers, one skis at first along the brook and then begins a steady climb as the trail pulls away from the brook. At 2.3 mi. one rounds a sharp switchback to the R, the most challenging part of the descent. A few hundred yards above this switchback the grade eases, but one continues a gradual ascent to a third crossing of Calamity Brook at 2.9 mi.

At this crossing there is a suspension bridge just upstream, but under most conditions one can cross the brook on the ice below the bridge. After crossing the brook, the steady climb resumes. At 3.3 mi. the grade eases, followed by a series of short climbs and short, sharp descents. At 4.3 mi. the trail reaches the N end of Calamity Pond, where a short side trail to the L leads to the large stone monument placed here in memory of David Henderson. Henderson was the driving force in developing the 19th-century iron mining operation at Tahawus. In 1848 he was accidentally shot at this spot while scouting the possibility of constructing a dam at Flowed Lands. The purpose of this dam would have been to divert the waters of the Opalescent River down Calamity Brook to increase the water power available to the then-proposed forge at Upper Works.

From the N end of Calamity Pond, the trail swings R and climbs gradually to Calamity Lean-tos on the S side of Flowed Lands at 4.7 mi. The dam that once created this large lake was breached in 1981, but the open area remains and provides the fine views of Mt. Colden and the MacIntyre Range.

The hiking trail around the W side of Flowed Lands is not skiable, so to continue on to Lake Colden, ski down into the open area. After finding a spot to cross the channel of the Opalescent River, turn N and ski to the upper end of the open area at approximately 5.3 mi. The trail to Lake Colden is just to the R of the Opalescent River. The trail leads immediately past a lean-to on the L and then past a lean-to on the R in another 100 yds. At 5.5 mi. the trail comes to the bank of the Opalescent River at a point just above the confluence of the Opalescent and the outlet to Lake Colden. One now crosses the river and reaches the dam and bridge at Lake Colden at 5.6 mi. **ADK**

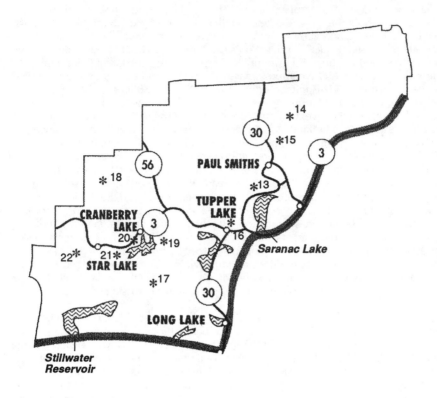

NORTHERN REGION

Novice
15. Hays Brook Truck Trail and the "Sheep Meadow"
17. Lake Lila
19. Burntbridge Pond Trail to Brandy Brook Flow
22. Streeter Lake via Aldrich Road

Novice–Intermediate
14. DeBar Game Management Area
18. Lampson Falls–Grass River trails

Intermediate
13. St. Regis Canoe Area
16. Old Wawbeek Road–Deer Pond Loop
17. Frederica Mt.
20. Peavine Swamp Trail
21. High Falls of the Oswegatchie

NORTHERN REGION

Compared to the High Peaks region, this region sees relatively little skier traffic; but that is not for a lack of opportunities. The trips described below are only a few of the many possibilities. The terrain in the Northern Region is generally flatter than other parts of the Adirondacks, but the multitude of lakes, rivers, and open wetlands offer their share of views—especially when one can ski right out to the middle to enjoy the full panorama.

Snowfall amounts vary widely, with the Cranberry Lake, Tupper Lake, and Paul Smiths areas often having bountiful snow even when the St. Lawrence Valley and Plattsburgh have bare ground. There are no commercial cross-country ski centers in this region, although the Adirondack Park Visitor Interpretive Center in Paul Smiths (the "VIC," as it is often known) has approximately 15 km of trail with loops for all abilities. The VIC does groom these loops on a limited basis, but there is no set track and no rentals or lessons available. The VIC also offers parking, warming, and restroom facilities along with interpretive displays on the Adirondacks. There is no trail fee. The VIC is also the northern end of a 9 mi. section of the Jackrabbit Trail that leads south to Lake Clear Junction. Check at the VIC for a map and conditions, and see trip #4 in this guide for more details about the Jackrabbit Trail.

The VIC is open seven days a week, excepting Thanksgiving and Christmas. For information on VIC programs or for snow conditions in the area, the number is (518) 327-3000. For snow conditions in the Tupper Lake area, call the Chamber of Commerce of Tupper Lake at (518) 359-3328.

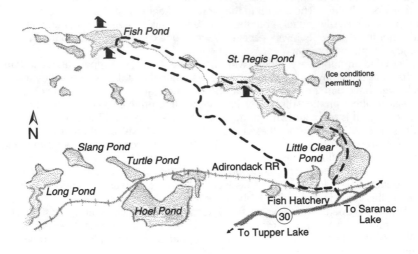

St. Regis Canoe Area (13)

13. ST. REGIS CANOE AREA

Distance: 11.6 mi., round-trip to Fish Pond; 6.5 mi., loop trip to St. Regis and Little Clear Ponds
Difficulty: Intermediate
ADK Guide and Map: Northern Region
USGS Maps: St. Regis 15′ or St. Regis Mt. and Upper Saranac Lake metric series

By far the most popular skiing in the region, the St. Regis Canoe Area offers a graded truck trail to Fish Pond with numerous variations using the lakes and portages connecting them. When the weather is fair and surface conditions suitable, most skiers prefer part of their trip to be on the open lake; but if this is not the case the truck trail offers excellent skiing and some of the most reliable snow in the Adirondacks.

The start is just off Rt. 30 on the side road that runs through the Adirondack Fish Hatchery. This road is 11.3 mi. N of the junction of Rtes. 30 and 3, or 2.3 mi. S of the junction of Rtes. 30 and 186. A DEC sign just W of the hatchery marks the winter trailhead (0 mi.), and there is usually ample room to park on the road. Begin by skiing 200 yds. to the abandoned railroad tracks. After crossing the tracks, turn L at the sign for Fish Pond. (Road straight ahead leads to Little Clear Pond.) The truck trail parallels the tracks for 0.7 mi. before turning R and down to the gate and register at 0.9 mi. At first mostly on the level, the truck trail begins climbing gently at 2.1 mi., levels off and then climbs moderately to a crest at 2.7 mi. The descent is to a junction at 3.3 mi. with a road leading R to St. Regis Pond.

(To do the 6.5-mi. loop trip, turn R, follow the road 0.2 mi. to the small dam on St. Regis Pond, and then ski to the far SE corner to find the portage trail. Marked with a white sign, this trail leads 0.5 mi. to Little Clear Pond. Complete the loop by skiing generally along the R shore, around a point, and on to the boat-launch site at the S end of the pond. From here a short climb leads to the starting point.)

Continuing on the truck trail, an unmarked trail to Grass Pond diverges L at 3.5 mi., and a portage to Ochre Pond goes R at 3 .7 mi. After several more short climbs and descents, the truck trail reaches the SE shore of Fish Pond at 5.8 mi. One lean-to is located about one-third of the way along the S shore while a second is located midway on the N shore. The usual return is via the truck trail, but a return of similar length, though more difficult, is possible by following the series of portages to Mud, Ochre, and St. Regis ponds. **ADK**

DeBar Game Management Area (14)
Based on DeBar Mt. & Meacham Lake quadrangles

14. DEBAR GAME MANAGEMENT AREA

Distances: 3.0 mi., round-trip Rt. 99 to Game Management Area; 9.0 mi., round-trip Beaver Valley loop; 10.2 mi., point-to-point Rt. 99 to Meacham Lake
Difficulty: Novice–Intermediate
ADK Guide and Map: Northern Region
USGS Maps: Debar Mt. 7.5' and Meacham Lake 7.5'

Characterized by relatively flat terrain, this remote area offers a number of interesting skiing possibilities and is often blessed with snow when nearby areas aren't. Since all of the trips described here are on old roads, this area is skiable with a minimum of snow cover. The VIC at Paul Smiths is the closest place to call for ski condition information. This area still sees some snowmobile traffic, but the signs placed in earlier years by snowmobilers are now gone and the roads are essentially unmarked. In recent years there has been some logging activity that has resulted in the first 1.4 mi. of this tour being plowed, but not sanded. Public access is still permitted, and on most days it is still possible (if not ideal) to ski on the road until the tour enters state land at 1.5 mi.

The start is the crossing of Hatch Brook on the remote and twisting Rt. 99, 10.9 mi. NW from Rt. 3, or 9.0 mi. SE of Rt. 30 at Duane. (The Meacham Lake end is on Rt. 30, 5.7 mi. S of Duane or 3.0 mi. N of the junction with Rt. 458.)

The trip starts on an unplowed road (0 mi.), which leads to a large open field at 1.5 mi. The views from this field are spectacular and it makes a destination in itself. To continue, proceed to the S end of the field, where there is a choice of three roads . The middle road leads to Meacham Lake, the left road is the return from the Beaver Valley Loop. (The slightly overgrown right road joins the route to Meacham Lake in approx. 0.5 mi.) Now gently rolling, the road reaches a junction at 4 mi. (Road L is the Beaver Valley trip leading E to a small impoundment and then up and N and back to the large field.)

Continuing past the junction, the road gradually swings to the W and climbs gently to a junction at 6.3 mi. with the East Mt. Trail. Continuing on, the road passes Winnebago Pond and then gently descends to a junction with the Debar Mt. Trail at 7.8 mi. From here the route is marked with standard red DEC markers to the Meacham Lake Campground at 9.0 mi. Since the campground roads are not plowed, continue past the entrance booth and swing R on Meacham Lake Road to reach Rt. 30 at 10.2 mi. **ADK**

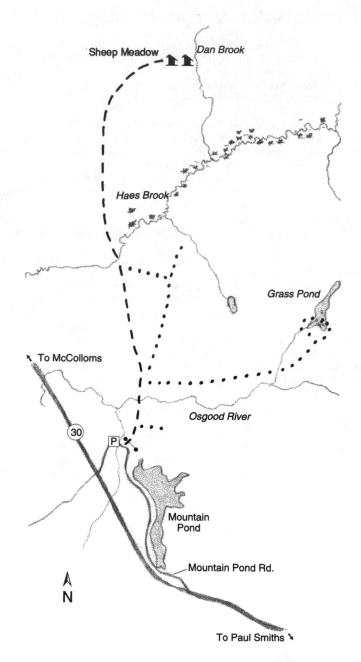

Sheep Meadow

Dan Brook

Haes Brook

Grass Pond

To McColloms

Osgood River

30

P

Mountain
Pond

Mountain Pond Rd.

N

To Paul Smiths

Hays Brook Truck Trail and the "Sheep Meadow" (15)
Based on St. Regis & Meacham Lake quadrangles

# 15. HAYS BROOK TRUCK TRAIL AND THE "SHEEP MEADOW"

Distance: 7.0 mi.
Difficulty: Novice
ADK Guide and Map: Northern Region
USGS Maps: St. Regis, 15' or St. Regis Mt. metric series and Meacham Lake, 7.5'

The "sheep meadow" is but one of several destinations possible in this area; all offer not only easy skiing but usually bountiful snow. The views from the meadow plus the two lean-tos make this the most popular destination. The start is at the N end of Mountain Pond off Rt. 30, 3.8 mi. N of the junction of Rt. 86 in Paul Smiths, and 5.4 mi. S of the junction of Rt. 458. The start is marked by a large DEC sign. There are both horse and snowmobile markers on the trail, but snowmobiles are rarely encountered .

Following the truck trail N from the gate (0 mi.), one crosses the Osgood River at 0.5 mi., after which the marked route leaves the truck trail going L and up. (Just beyond this junction the unmarked trail goes R to Grassy Pond, which is another interesting destination, reached 1.4 mi. from the truck trail.) It is also possible to stay on the truck trail, make a sharp L after 0.6 mi., and rejoin the marked route to the Sheep Meadow at 1.5 mi. After rejoining the truck trail, the trip crosses Hays Brook, climbs a short pitch, and levels out at 1.8 mi., after which it is mostly level to the lean-tos at 3.6 mi. **ADK**

Old Wawbeek Road-Deer Pond Loop (16)
Based on Upper Saranac, Derrick, Tupper Lake, and Stony Creek

16. OLD WAWBEEK ROAD–DEER POND LOOP

Distance: 7.3 mi., round-trip
Difficulty: Intermediate
ADK Guide and Map: Northern Region
USGS Maps: Long Lake 15', and St. Regis 15'or Tupper Lake and Upper Saranac Lake metric series

Around 1985 the DEC designated these trails for cross-country skiing from their previous designation as snowmobile trails. There is still some snowmobile traffic on the Old Wawbeek Road, but the trails to Deer Pond are usually used only by skiers. Deer Pond itself is a beautiful destination, although the trails are a bit rough and steep in a few spots. The Old Wawbeek Road, the predecessor to the present Rt. 3, offers a total of about 4 mi. of novice skiing through an interesting variety of forests. The start, 0.8 mi. W of the junction of Rtes. 3 & 30 (known as Wawbeek Corners), is marked by a sign for Deer Pond Cross-country Ski Area. Don't look for a base lodge or any grooming equipment, but this start does offer the best parking. The skiing is generally easier if the loop is done clockwise.

From the parking lot (0 mi.), bear L and follow the wide and gently rolling Old Wawbeek Road for 2.5 mi. to the junction with the red-marked DEC trail to Deer and Lead ponds. Turn R and up through a thick plantation of Norway spruce to a beaver pond at 2. 9 mi., followed by Mosquito Pond on the L and a steady climb to a ridge crest. The descent is steep for a few yards to the S end of Deer Pond at 4.2 mi. (An approximate 1.5-mi. side trip to Lead Pond is possible by skiing to the N end of Deer Pond and rejoining the red-marked trail.)

From the S end of Deer Pond the trail goes E to a junction with a yellow-marked trail. Turning R on this trail, one encounters a series of moderate to steep descents to a boggy area at 5.0 mi. after which the way is flat to the junction with the Wawbeek Truck Trail at 5.6 mi. (The road straight ahead leads in 0.7 mi. to Rt. 30 at a point 1.9 mi. N of Wawbeek Corners.) Turn R and enjoy a flat 1.2-mi. ski to the starting point. **ADK**

Lake Lila and Frederica Mt. (17)

17. LAKE LILA AND FREDERICA MT.

Distance: 15 mi., round-trip (plus 3 mi. to Frederica Mt.)
Difficulty: Novice (Intermediate to Frederica Mt.)
ADK Guide and Map: Northern Region
USGS Maps: Big Moose 15', Tupper Lake 15', and Wolf Mt. 7.5' or Little Tupper Lake, Beaver River, and Forked Lake metric series with Wolf Mt. 7.5'

As was written in the ADK's 1982 ski guide, "Lake Lila is a near-perfect destination for a ski tour [with] less than perfect means of access on skis." This statement still applies today because the summer access road may still be used for logging during the winter, but logging operations are now less than they once were. When logging is in progress, private vehicles are prohibited and skiing is not ideal on the plowed/rutted road. The alternative approach is via the abandoned Adirondack Railway line from Sabattis, but this route sees heavy snowmobile traffic. In spite of these access problems, it's worth making the effort to get there—perhaps during mid-week when snowmobile traffic is light.

Both approaches start on the Sabattis road which leaves Rt. 30 approximately 11.5 mi. S of the village of Tupper Lake and 10 mi. N of Long Lake. The summer access road is 7.7 mi. from Rt. 30. If not plowed due to logging operations, this road (though slightly longer than the railroad approach) is the preferred access, leading 5.8 mi. to a barrier gate from which a trail leads 0.3 mi.to the N shore of Lake Lila. If ice conditions are not favorable, continue on the road around the W shore of the lake to a junction with a road at 8.4 mi. leading up to the Nehasane station on the abandoned railroad.

If the summer access road is plowed, continue on Sabattis Rd. to the railroad at the end of the road 11 mi. from Rt. 30. Ski S on the railroad to Nehasane station, located just past milepost 88 (the "H" on each milepost indicates distance from Herkimer, the original southern terminus of the line). From the station, a road leads moderately down to the shore of Lake Lila at 7.5 mi. from Sabattis. The side trip to Frederica Mt. begins 0.2 mi. back towards the railroad and is marked with yellow markers. It follows a road that goes S, turns W and climbs to cross the tracks in 0.5 mi., and then continues to climb in stages to a junction at 1 mi. Here the trail to Frederica Mt. goes R and climbs steadily to the summit, 1.5 mi. from Lake Lila. The summit offers extensive views to the E and S, including the High Peaks nearly 50 mi. distant. **ADK**

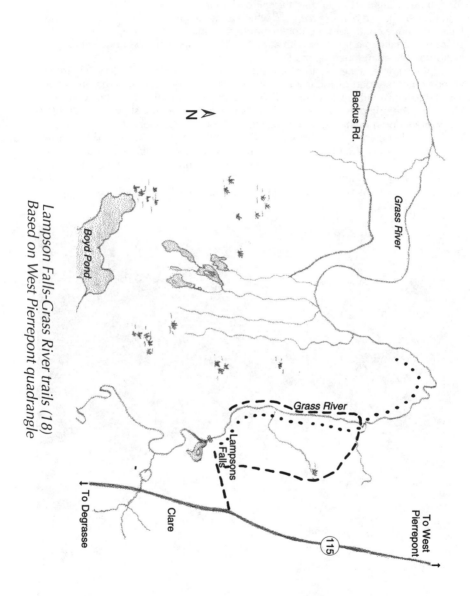

Lampson Falls-Grass River trails (18)
Based on West Pierrepont quadrangle

18. LAMPSON FALLS–GRASS RIVER TRAILS

Distance: 0.8 mi. - 7.6 mi., round-trip (depending on destination and side trips)
Difficulty: Novice–Intermediate
ADK Guide and Map: Northern Region
USGS Map: West Pierrepont 7.5'

This area offers a number of possible routes and destinations, with Lampson Falls the scenic highlight. It can be viewed from two vantage points with some nice skiing in between. The start is on Clare Rd. (County Rt. 115), 4.5 mi. from its intersection with County Rtes. 38 and 77 in the hamlet of Degrasse. From the road (0 mi.), pass around a gate and follow the old road, marked with red markers, 0.4 mi. to the head of Lampson Falls. Below the falls, the marked trail has a few small bridges out, so the better ski route veers R just before the falls and follows an old logging road that runs 100-200 yds. back from the river to a bridge across the
Grass River at 1.4 mi. The red markers now lead back up the opposite bank to a bluff with a view of Lampson Falls at 2.6 mi. Another possibility (requiring deeper than average snow cover however) is to turn R after crossing the bridge and continue downstream on the yellow-marked Cascades Trail past a series of smaller falls and flumes for 1.2 mi. to the end of the trail. **ADK**

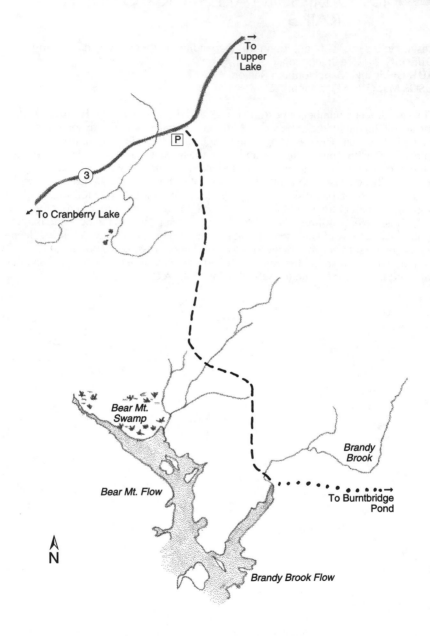

Burntbridge Pond Trail to Brandy Brook Flow (19)
Based on Cranberry Lake quadrangle

19. BURNTBRIDGE POND TRAIL TO BRANDY BROOK FLOW

Distance: 5.8 mi., round-trip
Difficulty: Novice
ADK Guide and Map: Northern Region
USGS Map: Cranberry Lake 7.5′

Following a DEC snowmobile trail along the remains of an old railroad grade, this trip affords novices a moderately long tour on flat terrain to the shore of Cranberry Lake. Not too many years ago, the more adventurous could usually find solitude by continuing beyond Brandy Brook Flow to Burntbridge Pond, but a new snowmobile trail connection between Conifer and Cranberry Lake has significantly increased the vehicular traffic from the lake shore to Burntbridge Pond. Since most all of the snowmobile traffic seems to head across the ice to Cranberry Lake village, the first part of this trail still offers some nice skiing with relatively little competition from vehicles.

The trail starts on Rt. 3, approximately 2 mi. E of the village of Cranberry Lake. Proceeding mostly on the level, the trail reaches an open meadow at 1.5 mi., a beaver pond at 2.1 mi. and then a bridge over Brandy Brook at 2.6 mi. From here it briefly follows the brook before veering L to an open glade on Brandy Brook Flow, one of many flooded inlets around Cranberry Lake, at 2.9 mi. For most skiers this will be the turnaround point, but the more adventurous can (if surface conditions are favorable) bear L and ski up all or part of the 1.5-mi. gradual grade to enjoy a run back down. Burntbridge Pond itself is over 2 mi. more of mostly flat skiing before coming to the new lean-to on the shore of the pond at 6.7 mi. **ADK**

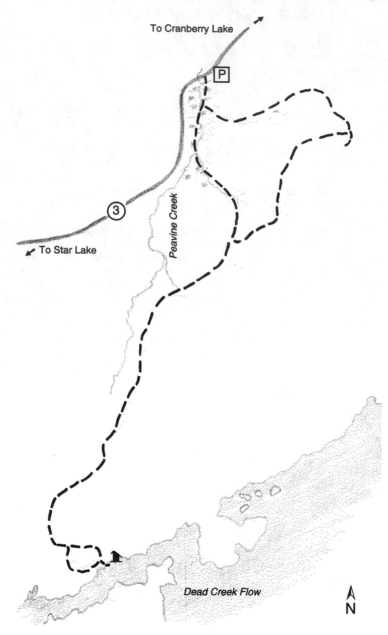

To Cranberry Lake

P

③

To Star Lake

Peavine Creek

Dead Creek Flow

N

Peavine Swamp Trail (20)
Based on Newton Falls and Cranberry Lake quadrangles

20. PEAVINE SWAMP TRAIL

Distance: 8.2 mi., round-trip
Difficulty: Intermediate
ADK Guide and Map: Northern Region
USGS Maps: Cranberry Lake 7.5' and Newton Falls 7.5'

This newly constructed trail runs from Rt. 3 along the edge of an extensive swamp before climbing a low ridge and ending at a secluded lean-to on the shore of Cranberry Lake. The trail is now officially marked as a ski trail by DEC, meaning that no snowmobiles or other vehicles are permitted. There are also now two side loops called Balancing Rock Loop and Christmas Tree Loop, each about 2.5 mi. long.

The trail begins 1.2 mi. W of the bridge over the Oswegatchie River at the outskirts of Cranberry Lake village. The trail is flat for 0.5 mi. and then climbs to some undulating terrain before starting a steeper climb at 1.6 mi. Reaching the top of the steepest climb at 2.6 mi., the trail descends, joins an old logging road, and reaches a height of land at 3.0 mi. Now following the old road, the trail descends and reaches the lean-to at 4.1 mi. **ADK**

High Falls of the Oswegatchie (21)

 21. HIGH FALLS OF THE OSWEGATCHIE

Distance: 12.8 mi., round-trip
Difficulty: Intermediate
ADK Guide and Map: Northern Region
USGS Maps: Five Ponds and Newton Falls, 7.5'

Although this trip has seen some skier traffic in recent years, one should assume that trailbreaking will usually be necessary. The reward for all this work is a delightful trip through a variety of relatively easy terrain. The destination can perhaps be summed up as a remote gateway to still greater remoteness since beyond High Falls is the largest trailless area in the Adirondacks—a seldom visited region stretching S to Stillwater Reservoir and containing the largest stand of virgin timber in the Adirondacks.

The start is in the hamlet of Wanakena, reached via a side road from Rt. 3, 8 mi. W of Cranberry Lake and 6 mi. E of Star Lake. Bear R 0.8 mi. down the road from Rt. 3, cross the Oswegatchie River, and park just beyond the actual start of the truck trail on the R. From the gate (0 mi.) the truck trail provides easy skiing, crossing Skate Creek at 0.7 mi. and coming to a junction at 1.8 mi. Beyond this point the truck trail has been abandoned due to extensive beaver flooding.

Turning L, the trail climbs to a low pass at 2.1 mi. and then descends to a brook at 2.9 mi., after which a few gentle rolls lead down to a beaver pond and brook at 4.3 mi. The trail crosses and then parallels the brook until a sign at 4.5 mi. indicates a new route for the trail which reaches the old truck trail at 4.8 mi. Turning L, the trail soon reaches a junction with the Five Ponds trail leading R to a bridge across the Oswegatchie River, Five Ponds, Wolf Pond, and Sand Lake.

Continuing straight ahead on the old truck trail one soon approaches Glasby Creek. There may be extensive beaver flooding before reaching the bridge over the creek, and caution is advised if the ice appears thin. After the bridge, the truck trail soon reaches a junction with the Plains Trail at 5.4 mi. Bearing R at this junction, the trail continues on the level to High Falls at 6.4 mi.

IMPORTANT NOTES:

1) Due to the July, 1995 microburst, the tour as described to High Falls remains impassable as of the summer of 1996. Work is progressing on a plan to reopen the old truck trail that reaches High Falls on a longer route by way of High Rock. Watch for an update in the ADK's *Adirondac* magazine or call the DEC's Canton office at (315) 386-4546 for current conditions. Skiers can reach High Falls via Dead Creek Flow, Sand Hill Junction, and The Plains trails. The only problem is about 0.25 mi. of steep terrain is north of Sand Hill Junction. All of these trails on this alternate have been cleared and are described in ADK's *Guide to Adirondack Trails - Northern Region.*

2) The road to Streeter Lake is clear, but it is not possible to continue beyond Tamarack Creek south of Crystal Lake due to the blowdown. **ADK**

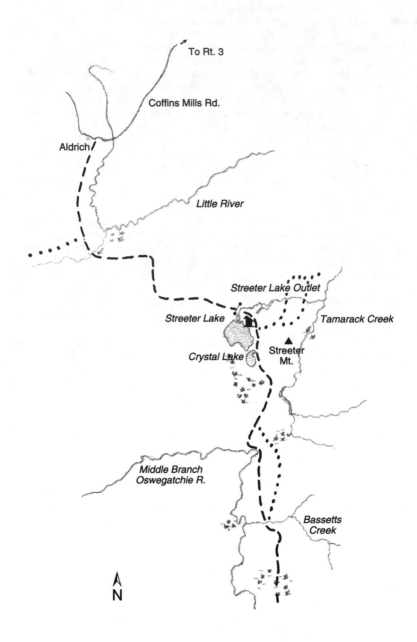

To Rt. 3

Coffins Mills Rd.

Aldrich

Little River

Streeter Lake Outlet

Streeter Lake

Tamarack Creek

Crystal Lake

Streeter Mt.

Middle Branch
Oswegatchie R.

Bassetts
Creek

N

Streeter Lake via Aldrich Road (22)
Based on ADK Northern Region map

22. STREETER LAKE VIA ALDRICH ROAD

Distance: 12.2 mi., round-trip (20 mi. with Totten–Crossfield Trail)
Difficulty: Novice
ADK Guide and Map: Northern
USGS Maps: Oswegatchie 7.5′ and Oswegatchie SE 7.5′

This is but one of several opportunities for long, relatively easy ski trips in this part of the Adirondacks. As the largest of the remote lakes, Streeter Lake makes a good destination. The Totten–Crossfield Trail offers a view of the remote Middle Branch of the Oswegatchie River and an historically important land corner as its final destination. One can also approach Streeter Lake from Star Lake via the Youngs Road approach, but the unplowed road from Aldrich is both easier to ski and to follow. The Amo Road approach has been officially abandoned.

To reach the Aldrich Road start, turn S off Rt. 3, 2 mi. W of Star Lake at a blinking traffic light. Turn L at a 'T' intersection 200 yds. from Rt. 3, and in another 0.2 mi. turn R on Coffin Mills Rd. This is followed 3.2 mi. to the unplowed Aldrich Road, found on the L just after the bridge over Little River. There will probably be some snowmobile tracks on this road for the 5.6 mi. to an old wooden gate at the former entrance to the Schuler family estate. Continuing on, there is a metal barrier at the outlet to Streeter Lake, and at 6.1 mi. is a large open field known as the "potato patch," where experimental potatoes were once raised for the family potato chip business.

The unmarked Totten–Crossfield Trail begins by following an old jeep road found at the S end of the field. Pass by the Streeter Lake Lean-to and the foundations of some houses to a junction with a road coming in from the L at 6.7 mi. Turn R at this jct. Another jct. is encountered at 6.9 mi. with the road R going to Crystal Lake. Turn L here and continue with a trail branching L to Tamarack Creek at 7.3 mi. followed by a beaver dam at 7.6 mi. The Francis Hill Trail goes L at 8.0 mi. after which the jeep road reaches a wide loop of the Middle Branch of the Oswegatchie at 8.3 mi. At 9.5 mi. the Francis Hill Trail rejoins the jeep road, which then crosses Bassett Creek at 8.5 mi. and ends at a roughly circular log landing at 8.8 mi.

Several trails radiate from this clearing. To reach the county line and the Totten and Crossfield stone marker, follow the log road straight ahead, which has recently been marked as a DEC horse and snowmobile trail. The county line is reached at 9.9 mi. The survey marker appears shortly before the county line in a small clearing on the R.

In 1771, Totten and Crossfield were the first to purchase a part of the interior Adirondacks; and in 1772 Archibald Campbell was commissioned to survey the boundary of their 800,000-acre tract. The line started north of the Mohawk River near Schenectady and ran northwest to this point. Here the boundary line turned east and then ran, theoretically at least, to a point 10 miles west of Lake Champlain. Then the line was to follow the Hudson or its tributaries south to the starting point. The latter part of this line remained theoretical, since Campbell abandoned the line at Coney Mt. south of Tupper Lake when, supposedly, "his rum supply ran out." Campbell did, however, establish this important corner to which are tied many county, town, and private property lines. Because of its significance, surveyor Verplanck Colvin in 1878 recovered Campbell's original marker and built the present and more substantial monument.

IMPORTANT NOTE: See p.57 for information regarding the July 1995 microburst and its affects on this trip. **ADK**

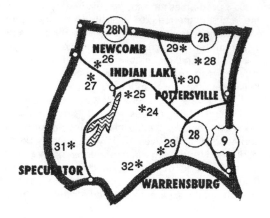

CENTRAL REGION

Novice
25. John Pond
29. Cheney Pond and Lester Flow
30. Stony Pond

Novice–Intermediate
32. Shanty Brook and Mud Ponds

Intermediate
23. East Branch of the Sacandaga Trail
24. Puffer Pond from Thirteenth Lake
26. Tirrell Pond from the South via Northville–Placid Trail
27. Stephens and Cascade ponds
28. Hoffman Notch
30. Stony Pond; intermediate for ski through to Irishtown
31. Pillsbury Lake

60

CENTRAL REGION

There are enough possibilities for cross-country skiing in this region that the ten described trips are but a small sampling of the tours one can do here. The region's centerpiece is the Siamese Ponds Wilderness Area, in which there are both short wilderness jaunts and long, rugged wilderness treks; but the outlying areas also offer a tremendous variety of ski terrain. Snowfall is generally plentiful in this region although the eastern edge along the Hudson River has significantly less snowfall than the rest of the region.

The only commercially developed cross-country ski centers are near North Creek. Garnet Hill Lodge is the most established operation, offering lodging as well as trails and direct access to several of the described tours. Cunningham's Ski Barn offers some interesting skiing near the Hudson River, while Gore Mt. maintains a few trails at the base of the downhill area. In addition to the commercial cross-country centers, the VIC in Newcomb has a few miles of trail and can give information on snow cover in the northern part of this region. Finally, the villages of Speculator (permit required on some trails) and Indian Lake maintain small loop trails for cross-country skiing.

Central Cross-country Ski Centers and Sites
Adirondack Hut to Hut Tours (518) 828-7007
Cunningham's Ski Barn (518) 251-3215
Garnet Hill Lodge (518) 251-2821
Gore Mt. Ski Center (518) 251-2411
Indian Lake (518) 648-5112
Speculator (518) 548-4521
Visitor Interpretive Center in Newcomb (518) 582-2000

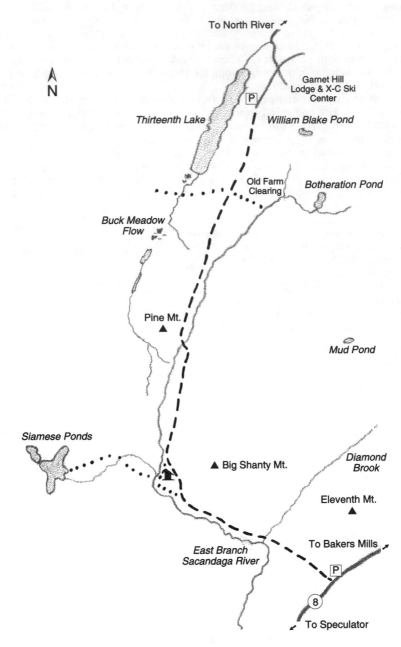

East Branch of the Sacandaga Trail (23)
Based on ADK Central Region map

23. EAST BRANCH OF THE SACANDAGA TRAIL

Distance: 11.1 mi., point-to-point
Difficulty: Intermediate
ADK Guide and Map: Central Region
USGS Maps: Thirteenth Lake 15' or Thirteenth Lake and Bakers Mills metric series

This challenging trip is certainly one of the classic wilderness traverses in the Adirondacks. Many skiers will elect to start at the S end, since it is easier to ascend the steep section next to Rt. 8 than to descend this 0.3 mi. on tired legs at the end of the trip. It is definitely possible, however, to ski down this section should the group desire to split up and arrange for an exchange of car keys in the middle. (One can also find easier skiing by following the unmarked and somewhat overgrown old stage road to the W of this steep section.) The other advantage in skiing from N to S is that much of the first 10 mi. is downhill rather than the other way around. The logistics involved in shuttling cars make a "key swap" plan attractive on this trip; but, as with any such arrangement, there should be two self-sufficient parties with contingency plans in the event of failure to meet up as planned.

The N end of this trip begins at the end of Thirteenth Lake Road, which leaves Rt. 28, just N of North River. A DEC sign for the Siamese Ponds Wilderness Area marks this turn along with signs for Garnet Hill Lodge. At 3.4 mi. from Rt. 28 bear L at a junction and then bear R at the next two junctions to reach a fair-sized parking area at the end of the plowed road. (The groomed ski trails in this area are maintained by Garnet Hill Lodge and require a trail fee.) Continue straight ahead to the gate at the boundary of the Siamese Ponds Wilderness Area.

The south end of this trip is on Rt. 8, 4.0 mi. W of Bakers Mills, at a large parking lot with a DEC sign. The trail begin s with a steep climb of 240 ft. to a col on the shoulder of Eleventh Mt. Here the route of the old stage road enters from the L, and the trail follows this route all the way to Thirteenth Lake. From the col, the trail descends gently to Diamond Brook at 1.5 mi. and then begins following the NE bank of the river up to Burnt Shanty Clearing at 2.7 mi. At 3.5 mi. one comes to a junction (a newer marked trail heads L and along the river to a lean-to and suspension bridge across the river for the Siamese Ponds Trail, but the connection beyond the lean-to is not as good for skiing as the original trail). Bearing R at 3.5 mi., the newer trail comes back i n at 4.3 mi., and the trail reaches Big Shanty Flow at 4.6 mi.

Continuing on near the flow, there is a large boulder on the R at 5.2 mi., a bridge across Cross Brook at 5.7 mi., and the crossing of the East Branch on a new bridge at 6.6 mi. At about 7.0 mi. there is a short climb followed by a level section and then two more distinctly steeper grades to a height to land at 8.9 mi. (With less than ideal snow, descending this section can be tricky due to some large rocks on the eroded grades.) From the height of land a gradual descent leads to the junction with the Puffer Pond Trail at 9.5 mi., followed by Old Farm Clearing at 9.6 mi. From here, easy skiing leads to the plowed end of Thirteenth Lake Rd. at 11.1 mi. **ADK**

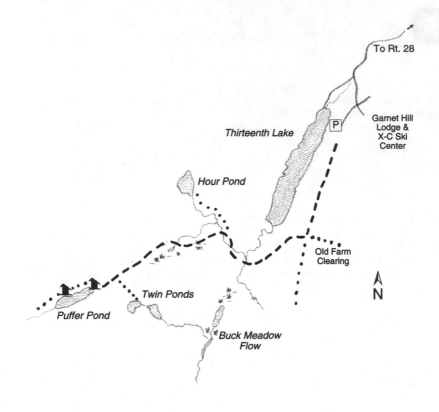

Puffer Pond from Thirteenth Lake (24)
Based on ADK Central Region map

24. PUFFER POND FROM THIRTEENTH LAKE

Distance: 11.0 mi., round-trip
Difficulty: Intermediate
ADK Guide and Map: Central Region
USGS Maps: Thirteenth Lake 15′ or metric series

Set between the steep slopes of Bullhead and Puffer mts., Puffer Pond is an attractive destination, whether approached from Thirteenth Lake or Kings Flow (via Puffer Pond Brook Trail.) The Thirteenth Lake approach is generally the most popular, and gives skiers the option of a side trip to Hour Pond. Crossing Hour Pond Outlet is potentially a problem, but a relatively short and easy bushwhack can bypass this problem. The start is the same as the northern start for the East Branch of the Sacandaga Trail (see trip # 23).

From the parking area (0 mi.), ski to the junction just beyond Old Farm Clearing at 1.6 mi. Turning R, the trail descends to cross an inlet to Thirteenth Lake at 2.5 mi., after which the trail begins to climb, parallels Hour Pond Outlet, and then crosses this brook at 2.8 mi. (If this crossing is not possible, continue up the bank of the brook for 150 yds. and then climb 40-50 vertical feet to a higher shelf, which is followed for another 200 yds. to a small brook. The Puffer Pond Trail is found just across this small brook.)

Assuming the crossing is feasible, at 2.9 mi. the trail reaches the junction with a trail leading R 1.2 mi. to Hour Pond—a charming destination in itself or a pleasant side trip. Continuing on, the Puffer Pond Trail recrosses Hour Pond Outlet and ascends rolling terrain to crest at 3.6 mi. From here there is a good view of Puffer Mt. After descending to an abandoned beaver dam and meadow at 3.7 mi., the trail climbs moderately for 150 yds., after which the terrain is mostly level to Puffer Pond at 5.5 mi. There is one lean-to at the E end and another 0.2 mi. along the N shore. **ADK**

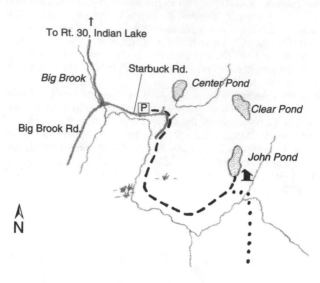

John Pond (25)
Based on ADK Central Region map

25. JOHN POND

Distance: 6.0 mi., round-trip
Difficulty: Novice
ADK Guide and Map: Central Region
USGS Map: Thirteenth Lake 15' or metric series

Combining an attractive destination with easy but not boring skiing, this trip has become quite popular in recent years. One can also make this an 8.0-mi. intermediate-level, point-to-point trip by starting at Kings Flow and proceeding via the Puffer Pond Trail and John Pond Crossover.

The start for John Pond is SE of the village of Indian Lake. From the intersection of Rtes. 28 and 30 in Indian Lake, proceed S on Rt. 30 0.6 mi. and turn L on Big Brook Rd. for 3.3 mi. to Starbuck Rd. Turn L for 0.4 mi. and bear L at the entrance to Wilderness Lodge. Now on Lake View Dr., proceed 0.5 mi. to a 'T' intersection where one turns R 0.2 mi. to the trailhead. (There may be vehicle tracks for another 0.1 mi. to the barrier, but the end of plowing is the best place to start. (Coming from the E on Rt. 28 , one can also reach Big Brook Rd. by turning L on Chamberlin Rd., County Rt. 18, at the top of a long hill, 1.0 mi. W of the sign announcing the Indian Lake town line.)

From the trailhead (0 mi.), the trail is gently rolling for 0.9 mi. to a fork where the John Pond Trail goes sharp L and continues to climb in generally easy stages. At 1.7 mi. a side trail L leads to the burial ground of Peter Savary and Eliza Emilia King, two children who died of diphtheria. At 2.7 mi. the John Pond Crossover Trail diverges to the R, after which the trail rises in several easy pitches to reach the lean-to at 3.0 mi. **ADK**

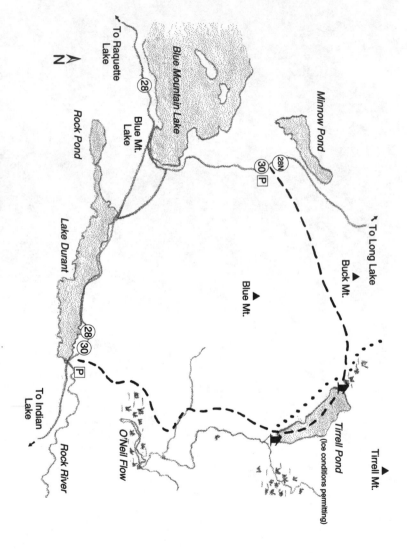

Tirrell Pond from the South via Northville–Placid Trail (26)
Based on ADK Central Region map

26. TIRRELL POND FROM THE SOUTH VIA NORTHVILLE–PLACID TRAIL

Distance: 7 mi., round-trip
Difficulty: Novice - Intermediate
ADK Guide and Map: Central Region
USGS Maps: Blue Mt. Lake 15' or Blue Mt. Lake and Deerland metric series

Long a favorite of winter campers because of its two lean-tos and wonderful scenery, Tirrell Pond has more recently become a favored destination for skiers. This trip follows the Northville-Placid Trail, which crosses Rtes. 28 and 30 2.6 mi. E of Blue Mt. Lake. The Tirrell Pond trip starts on the N side of the highway. (Across the road is the start for the Stephens Pond trip # 31.) From the trailhead (0 mi.), the trail climbs diagonally up a road cut to a trail register and then heads N following blue markers. At 0.6 mi. the trail bears L at a junction with a tote road and descends to cross two wet areas on good bridges. At 1.7 mi. the trail bears L and up, crossing a lumber road and then a brook at 1.9 mi. Here it turns sharp L to follow the N bank of the brook. Recrossing the brook twice, the trail climbs away from the brook and crosses a lumber road at 2.5 mi. Now the grade eases as the trail passes through a clearing, crosses another brook, and reaches a second clearing at 2.8 mi. A R turn and then a L turn on good roads are followed by a recently cut area and then back to state land at 3.4 mi. O'Neil Flow Lean-to is reached at 3.5 mi. at the S end of the pond.

One can also reach Tirrell Pond from the trailhead 0.1 mi. N of the Adirondack Museum in Blue Mt. Lake. This route is approximately one mile longer, and the descent to Tirrell Pond from the height of land N of Blue Mt. requires a bit more than intermediate skill. However, starting at Blue Mt. Lake and skiing to the Northville-Placid Trail start is a nice 8-mi. trip with a net descent of over 400 vertical feet. **ADK**

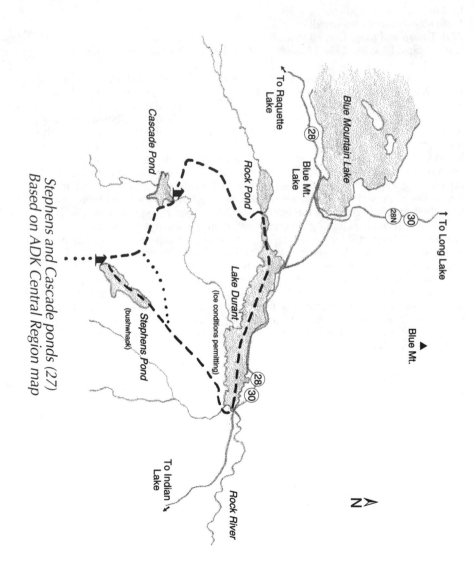

Stephens and Cascade ponds (27)
Based on ADK Central Region map

27. STEPHENS AND CASCADE PONDS

Distance: 6.6 mi., Stephens Pond round-trip; 8.8 mi., loop trip to both ponds
Difficulty: Intermediate
ADK Guide and Map: Central Region
USGS Maps: Blue Mt. Lake 15′ or Blue Mt. Lake metric series

There are many variations to these described trips depending on the inclination of the group and the condition of the ice on Lake Durant. If the ice conditions are good, one can make this a loop trip starting at Lake Durant Public Campground (although 1.8 mi. can be saved with a shuttle to Durant Rd. at the W end of the lake). Lake Durant Public Campground is on Rtes. 28 and 30, 2.6 mi. E of Blue Mt. Lake and approx. 8 mi. W of Indian Lake.

From the parking lot (0 mi.), ski W on the ice to the outlet of Rock Pond at 2.4 mi. at the W end of the lake. Here one encounters the Cascade Pond Trail, which goes L, and with a bit of steep going both up and down, gets over a ridge before turning W and up a beautiful valley. The trail steepens again at 3.6 mi., after which it levels out and swings E to the lean-to at the outlet of Cascade Pond at 4.6 mi. If ice conditions permit, the easiest route from the lean-to is to ski to the far end of the east bay of the pond. From there, it is an easy 100 yd. bushwhack up to the trail. Otherwise, follow the markers across the outlet after which the trail is at first level and then climbs to a junction with the Northville-Placid Trail (trail register) at 5.5 mi.

From here, one can turn L and return 2.7 mi. to the starting point, but turning R one descends to the lean-to on Stephens Pond at 6.1 mi. Again assuming ice conditions are favorable, one can return by skiing to the N end of Stephens Pond, from which a 1/4-mi. bushwhack up a wide, gentle, and obvious valley leads to the Northville-Placid Trail at 7.0 mi. The trail now descends in gradual stages to Lake Durant at 8.8 mi. **ADK**

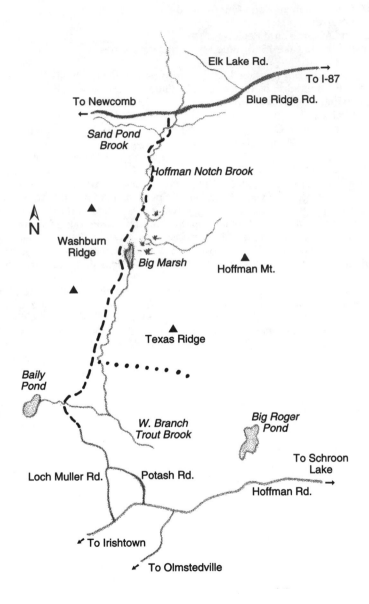

Hoffman Notch (28)

28. HOFFMAN NOTCH

Distance: 7.6 mi., round-trip to Big Marsh; 7.4 mi., through trip to Blue Ridge Rd. (see cautions)
Difficulty: Novice–Intermediate to Big Marsh; Intermediate beyond
ADK Guide and Map: Central Region
USGS Maps: Schroon Lake 15' or Blue Ridge and Schroon Lake metric series

With steep ridges rising on both sides, Hoffman Notch offers some of the most spectacular scenery available to skiers in the Adirondacks. This route was once marked as a snowmobile trail, but this use ended after the area was designated as wilderness. Since then, maintenance has been spotty—especially N of Big Marsh—so that those attempting a through trip may have difficulty with blowdown. In addition, the descent on the N side of the notch has three stream crossings without bridges, and the trail has not been brushed out to the full width of the original road, leaving less room to maneuver. The difficult crossing of the beaver swamp, however, has been replaced by 1 mi. of new trail that swings to the W of the old trail. Coming from Blue Ridge Road, the new trail diverges R 0.1 mi. from the road and rejoins the old trail at the crossing of the power line 1.1 mi. from the road. There is no immediate plan to further improve the rest of the trail N of Big Marsh. For some, this lack of amenities makes this end of the trip "true" wilderness and therefore all the more desirable; but most skiers will find enough wild scenery with the trip as described to Big Marsh.

The start is at the tiny cluster of houses known as Loch Muller. From Rt. 9 at the S end of the village of Schroon Lake, take Hoffman Rd. 5.6 mi. W to the junction of Loch Muller Rd. Turn R and proceed 2.4 mi. to an old white hotel building after which the plowing usually ends. (If it does appear the plowing is adequate beyond here, go 0.1 mi. and then turn R for another 0.1 mi. to a turnout with a DEC sign marking the start.) From the DEC sign (0 mi.) the trail begins by descending to the West Branch of Trout Brook (Bailey Pond outlet) at 0.4 mi. The trail crosses the brook on a new bridge and then climbs across the S slope of Washburn Ridge. After crossing several small brooks, the trail descends to the W bank of the North Branch of Trout Brook at 1.2 mi.

Here a trail leads R across a new foot bridge. This is an old snowmobile trail, now reopened as a foot path, leading to Big Pond. Under most snow conditions it is too rough to ski. (Many skiers coming from the N end have become confused here as this trail appears to be the route to Loch Muller as shown—incorrectly—on the 1953 USGS map.)

Bearing L at this jct. (R if coming from the N), the Hoffman Notch trail now generally follows the bottom of a flat valley with much fresh beaver activity. At 3.8 mi. the trail reaches the W shore of Big Marsh—in reality a sizable pond. From the surface of the pond there are excellent views of Texas Ridge, Hornet Cobbles, and Washburn Ridge.

For those continuing beyond Big Marsh, the going is flat for another 0.8 mi. to Hoffman Notch Brook. From here one is faced with several potentially difficult brook crossings along with 500 ft. of vertical descent before reaching the Blue Ridge Rd. This trailhead is on the S side of the road just W of a bridge over The Branch, 5.7 mi. from Northway Exit 29 and 13.2 from NY 28N and the Tahawus Road. **ADK**

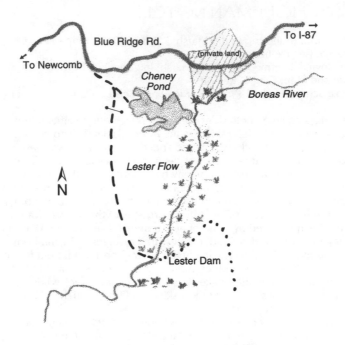

Cheney Pond and Lester Flow (29)
Based on ADK Central Region map

29. CHENEY POND AND LESTER FLOW

Distance: 5.2 mi., round-trip
Difficulty: Novice
ADK Guide and Map: Central Region
USGS Maps: Schroon Lake 15' or Blue Ridge metric series

Relatively easy skiing combined with some unusual views of the Great Range make this a great little trip. It is, however, a long drive from just about anywhere and at times there can be moderate snowmobile use. Nevertheless, the view from the south end of Lester Flow makes this a worthwhile trip despite these potential problems. While once one could usually return via the ice on Lester Flow, the old dam at Lester Flow has now been breached and the current in the Boreas River makes it far less likely that ice conditions will be good enough to permit a return back up the open flow.

The start is on Blue Ridge Rd., 5.5 mi. N and then E from Rt. 28N and 13.5 mi. W from Northway Exit 29. From Blue Ridge Rd. (0 mi.), the road descends gradually to an intersection at 0.4 mi. (The road L goes 0.3 mi. to Cheney Pond.)

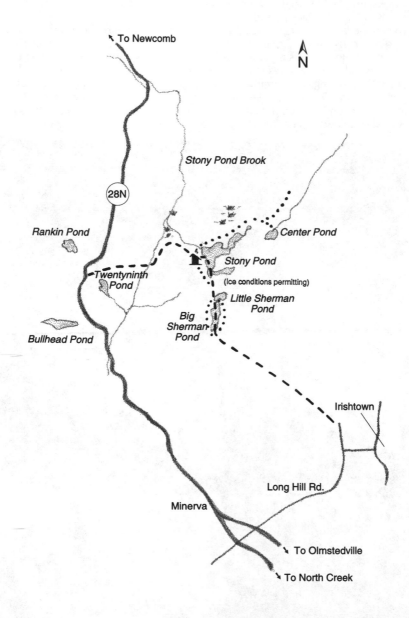

Stony Pond (30)
Based on ADK Central Region map

Bearing R, the route to Lester Flow dam soon reaches a barrier and then an unmarked junction at 0.5 mi. Bear L and continue mostly on the level until a long, gradual descent leads to a large beaver dam on the R at 2.4 mi. Turning L at a junction at 2.5 mi., the route leads through a small campsite to the edge of Lester Flow at 2.6 mi. Looking to the N, one can see the Great Range with the bare rock faces of Basin and Gothics prominent.

When the large crib dam was in use, it created the large body of water shown on the older maps. Now there is only a small bit of slack water above the old dam and the former flow area is rapidly growing up. It is usually possible, however to obtain an even better view by crossing the Boreas River to the rocky bluffs on the E side; pick the crossing spot carefully as there is considerable current in the river that can cause thin ice. If one does attempt the trip back up the open flow and across Cheney Pond, most if not all the skiing should be in the thick alders and occasional meadows beside the river until one reaches Cheney Pond. **ADK**

Pond on Three Ponds Mt.

Lance King

30. STONY POND

Distance: 4.2 mi., round-trip ; 6.0 mi., point-to-point
Difficulty: Novice (Intermediate for through ski)
ADK Guide and Map: Central
USGS Maps: Newcomb 15' and Schroon Lake 15' or Newcomb and Blue Ridge metric series

The trips as described below are but two of several excellent possibilities in this area. There are several smaller ponds to explore, and Green Mt. can make a good destination for a ski/snowshoe trip. The through trip offers skiers over 900 ft. of net vertical descent, although a few short pitches are on the high side of intermediate. The start is on Rt. 28N, 3.9 mi. N of its junction with the Olmsteadville Rd. (To find the Irishtown end of the through trip, turn L, if coming from the N, off Rt. 28N on the Minerva–Olmsteadville Rd. and then L on Long Hill Rd. S of the center of Minerva. It is 1.7 mi to a junction, which one passes straight through to the E trailhead at 2.1 mi. from Minerva–Olmsteadville Rd.)

From the start on Rt. 28N (0 mi.), a cable barrier blocks the road that starts up a short grade and levels off with a trail going R at 0.3 mi. to a campsite and Twentyninth Pond. Just beyond, at 0.4 mi., bear L at a junction and come to a height of land at 0 .5 mi. after which there is a descent first to one brook crossing at 0.8 mi. and then to the bottom of the valley and another brook at 1 .0 mi. From here the trail climbs in stages past several beaver ponds to the lean-to on Stony Pond at 2.1 mi.

To continue through to Irishtown, ski to the S end of the pond and find the trail, which climbs slightly and then descends a short, steep, and somewhat difficult pitch to Little Sherman Pond at 2.8 mi. One can now ski to the S end of Big Sherman Pond and find the trail on the E shore near the outlet at 3.0 mi. Turning R at the junction with the trail that runs along the E shore, the descent to Irishtown soon begins. At 3.6 mi. yellow paint blazes indicate a small inholding of private land and a private trail going R. After a short, steep pitch at 4.3 mi. the steady grade resumes to the end of the trail at 6.0 mi. **ADK**

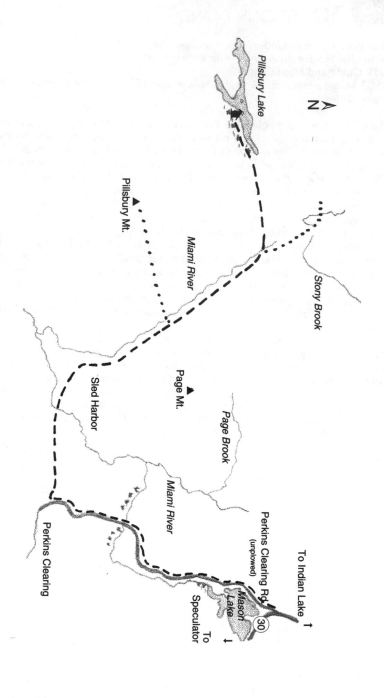

Pillsbury Lake (31)
Based on ADK Central Region map

31. PILLSBURY LAKE

Distance: 12.8–19.4 mi., (depending on plowing)
Difficulty: Intermediate
ADK Guide and Map: Central Region
USGS Maps: Indian Lake 15' and West Canada Lakes 15' or Page Mt. and West Canada Lakes metric series

In recent years, the 3.3 mi. of road from Mason Lake to Perkins Clearing has not been plowed, so reaching Pillsbury Lake is likely to be a very long day trip. Nevertheless, Pillsbury Lake is a worthy objective with enjoyable skiing along the way, so that one's day is not totally wasted if the destination is not reached. The start is on Rt. 30, 8.2 mi. N of Speculator and 4.0 mi. S of the bridge over Lewey Lake outlet. If the road is not plowed, there will likely be snowmobile tracks for the 3.3 mi. to Perkins Clearing, as this is part of the Indian Lake/Speculator snowmobile trail system. (Be aware that the snowmobile trails lead in many directions with a variety of signs and markers, but only the DEC signs lead one to the Pillsbury Lake trail.)

Turning R on a road at Perkins Clearing, the route crosses the Miami River at 4.3 mi. and reaches a large open area known as Sled Harbor at 5.1 mi. Just beyond Sled Harbor, look for a sign and bear R following red markers. Grades are now mostly gentle to a barrier at 6.3 mi., at the junction where the Pillsbury Mt. Trail goes L.

Going straight ahead at the Pillsbury Mt. trail junction, follow the wider road, This steepens a bit at 6.9 mi. as it climbs to a height of land at 7.9 mi., where there is a junction. (Trail straight ahead leads 2.7 mi. to Cedar Lakes.) Turning L, the trail descends gently to a flatter area at 9.2 mi., and the short side trail leads 300 ft. to the lean-to on Pillsbury Lake at 9.7 mi. **ADK**

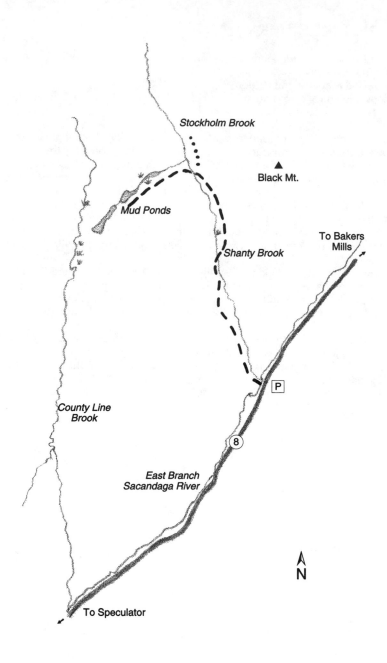

Stockholm Brook

Black Mt.

Mud Ponds

Shanty Brook

To Bakers
Mills

County Line
Brook

P

8

East Branch
Sacandaga River

N

To Speculator

Shanty Brook and Mud Ponds (32)
Based on ADK Central Region map

32. SHANTY BROOK AND MUD PONDS

Distance: 7.6 mi., round-trip
Difficulty: Novice–Intermediate
ADK Guide and Map: Central Region
USGS Maps: Thirteenth Lake 15' or Bakers Mills metric series

Despite their unappealing names, this trip's destination is a most attractive spot. Legend says that early guides would name their favorite fishing spots "mud pond" to discourage others from going there. When covered with snow and ice these ponds are even more attractive than in the summer, and the ski along Shanty Brook is an additional bonus. The only problem is crossing the East Branch of the Sacandaga at the beginning. At the ford, the river is wide but shallow; it should be crossable unless there has been a recent thaw, but do have an alternate trip in mind just in case.

The start is on Rt. 8, 10.1 mi. NE of the junction of Rtes. 8 and 30 and 8.4 mi. SE of Bakers Mills. There is a large turnoff at the trailhead. N of the turnoff is an old road that slants down towards the river. Two cables are the remains of a former bridge with the Shanty Brook Trail beginning on the N bank at these cables. (In winter, pick the best crossing and use these cables to easily locate the start.) From the N bank (0 mi.) the trail heads N and reaches Shanty Brook at 0.2 mi., follows it briefly, and then angles up a slope to a flatter section at 0.7 mi. (Just beyond, a vague trail leads R 100 yds. to Shanty Brook Falls.) Continuing on, the trail crosses Shanty Brook at 1.4 mi. with a large vlei encountered at 1.9 mi. Here the trail becomes vague, but one can find it again at the NE corner of the vlei after which the easiest skiing may be right up the brook to Mud Ponds—making sure to turn L at the junction with Stockholm Brook. If the brook is not skiable, the trail continues on with beaver meadows on the L, crosses a tributary brook at 2.4 mi. and then comes to an indistinct junction at 2.5 mi. An arrow carved into a grey birch points L here, down to a crossing of Shanty Brook with the marshy confluence of Shanty and Stockholm brooks reached at 2.7 mi. Here the trail swings W and up through generally open terrain to the shore of the first Mud Pond at 3.5 mi. The second pond is just beyond at 3.6 mi. (Those experienced at navigating off-trail can continue through this low pass and return down County Line Brook to that trailhead on Rt. 8, approx. 3.5 mi. SE of the starting point.) **ADK**

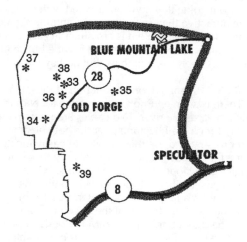

WEST-CENTRAL REGION

Novice
33. Cascade Lake

Novice–Intermediate
34. Big Otter Lake Truck Trail
36. Safford Pond

Intermediate
35. Inlet–Limekiln Lake Area
37. Panther Pond
38. Chub Lake
39. Gull Lake

WEST-CENTRAL REGION

Perhaps the most significant feature of the West-Central Region is that Old Forge usually leads the Adirondacks in total annual snowfall, with miles and miles of skiable terrain and trails leading to dozens of picturesque ponds. The area's only drawback, perhaps, is such an abundance of snowmobilers that skiers might begin to feel a close bond with some of the world's ethnic minorities. However, this region encompasses two of the Adirondacks' larger wilderness areas, Ha-de-ron-dah and Pigeon Lake, as well as numerous other trails on which motorized vehicles are prohibited. A few of the described tours do use snowmobile routes for all or part of their distance, but only on trails that experience has shown are lightly used for snowmobiling while offering good terrain for skiers. A quick glance at the map will show that there are many possibilities for ski tours beyond those described here, and the ADK 's current hiking guide to this region has information on suitable winter uses for most all of the trails in this region.

There are currently three developed areas for cross-country skiing in the Old Forge–Inlet Area. Adirondack Woodcraft is based at a summer camp, McCauley Mt. is part of a downhill ski center, and Fern Park is operated by the Town of Inlet.

West-Central Cross-country Ski Centers and Sites
Adirondack Woodcraft Ski Touring Center (315) 369-6031
Fern Park Recreation Area (315) 357-5501
McCauley Mountain (315) 369-3225

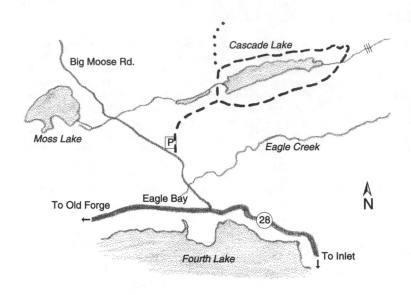

Cascade Lake (33)
Based on ADK West-Central Region map

 **33. CASCADE LAKE**

Distance: 2–5.6 mi., round-trip
Difficulty: Novice
ADK Guide and Map: West-Central Region
USGS Maps: Big Moose 15′ or Eagle Bay metric series

Offering easy skiing, a beautiful lake, a variety of possible distances, and a waterfall, this tour is an ideal introduction to the region. The start is on Big Moose Rd., 0.9 mi. W of Rt. 28 in Eagle Bay. There is a small parking area which is usually plowed. The actual trailhead register is about 100 ft. into the woods. One can head straight for it or find easier grades on an old road 100 ft. back towards Eagle Bay. The trail is marked with yellow DEC ski trail disks and an occasional red marker.

From the register (0 mi.) gentle grades, first up then down, lead to a junction at 0.8 mi., just before a large meadow. (If one's goal is just the 2.2-mi. tour to the lake and back, turn L at this junction and glide down to the outlet of Cascade Lake at 1.0 mi.) To make the complete circuit, bear R at this junction. At first the trail is mostly level across a slope before gently descending to a brook at 2.8 mi. (A short bushwhack up this brook brings one to a high, narrow waterfall from which the lake derives its name.) With less than perfect snow cover, it may be difficult to cross this major inlet to Cascade Lake or to cross several smaller streams just beyond. If the crossings are too difficult, one can always turn around; but under good conditions the continuation makes an enjoyable loop.

About 1 mi. after crossing the major brook, one comes to some overgrown fields, once part of a summer camp. This is followed by a beautiful open point with an outhouse for the designated campsite at 4.0 mi. At 4.5 mi. a red-marked trail diverges R, but bearing L the trail crosses the outlet to Cascade Lake at 4.6 mi. and then climbs gently up to the R of the open field to the junction with the trail one started on at 4.8 mi. Turn R to return to the road at 5.6 mi. **ADK**

Canada Lake

Lawrence King

85

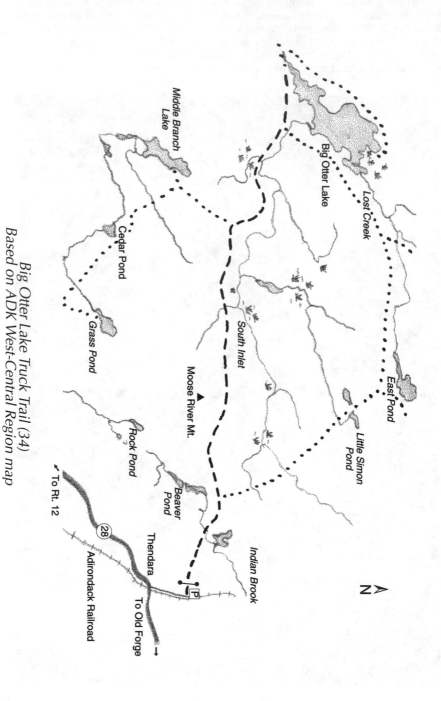

Big Otter Lake Truck Trail (34)
Based on ADK West-Central Region map

 **34. BIG OTTER LAKE TRUCK TRAIL**

Distance: up to 17.4 mi., round-trip
Difficulty: Novice–Intermediate
ADK Guide and Map: Central Region
USGS Maps: McKeever 15' or Thendara metric series

A few years ago, one of the major ski manufacturers adopted the slogan "as far as you want to go." In doing so they must have had this area in mind, because the gently rolling terrain traversed by this truck trail invites one to push on and on. Those who manage to ski all the way to Big Otter Lake will have crossed the Ha-de-ron-dah Wilderness Area and returned; but since crossing the wilderness only leads one to more snowmobile trails at the W end, there is no shame in settling for a round-trip ski to Indian Brook (3.0 mi.) or the high point on the side of Moose River Mt. (6.0 mi.). The obvious attractions of this tour have made it quite popular with skiers, and one may expect to have broken track for at least part of the way.

The start is in Thendara, on a side road leading N from Rt. 28 just W of the railroad underpass. Follow this road 0.4 mi. to its end, where there is a parking area. From the parking area (0 mi.), the route runs concurrently with a heavily used snowmobile trail for a few yards before turning L and up to a barrier gate and register at 0.3 mi. (Use caution descending this hill as snowmobile traffic can be heavy.) Past the barrier gate, a series of ups and downs lead to a longer descent to an open wetland at 1.0 mi. This is followed first by a crossing of Indian Brook and then the junction with the East Pond–Lost Creek Trail at 1.5 mi. Bearing L, the truck trail begins a gradual climb up a ridge, swinging R at 2.2 mi. and continuing a gentle climb across the slope with occasional views to the N. At 3.0 mi. the truck trail begins to descend and then flattens before reaching a junction with a trail L to Middle Branch and Middle Settlement Lakes at 4.9 mi. Bearing R, a short climb and descent lead to a large open area at 5.9 mi. and the jct. with the Lost Creek trail at 6.5 mi. Continuing on, the truck trail ends at 7.4 mi.

For skiers, the best route by which to continue from the end of the truck trail is an unmarked wood road going R just before the end of the truck trail and leading to Big Otter Lake at 7.5 mi. The Big Otter Lake East Trail continues as a footpath before reaching the W boundary of the wilderness area at 7.8 mi. (It is possible to continue via the Big Otter West Trail to a trailhead 3.7 mi. beyond Big Otter Lake to make a point-to-point tour of 11.2 mi.; but, given that more time would likely be spent in a very longshuttle, and that the W end is a frequently used snowmobile trail, this is not recommended.) **ADK**

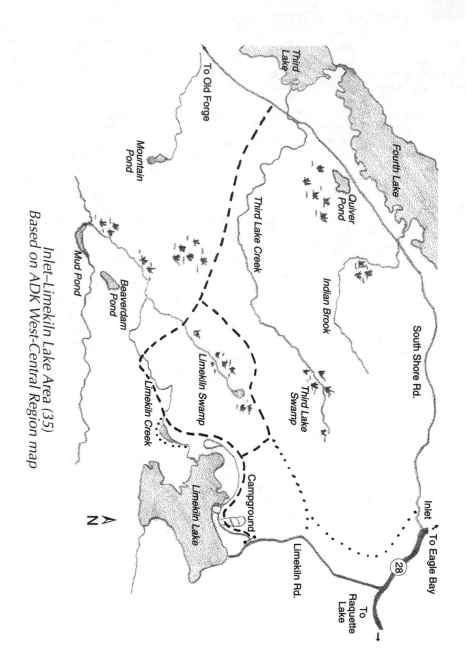

Inlet–Limekiln Lake Area (35)
Based on ADK West-Central Region map

# 35. INLET-LIMEKILN LAKE AREA

Distances: 7.1 mi., point-to-point; 7.0 mi., round-trip
Difficulty: Intermediate
ADK Guide and Map: West-Central Region
USGS Maps: Old Forge 15' or metric series

There are many possibilities for cross-country skiing around Inlet beyond the two variations described below. Other possibilities include incorporating the Town of Inlet's cross country ski center into a route for a longer tour, or perhaps just idling along the shore of Limekiln Lake on a campground road for an easy but scenic ski.

The start for this trip is at Limekiln Lake Campground, reached via a road that leaves Rt. 28 0.8 mi. E of the center of Inle t. The entrance to Limekiln Lake Campground is on the R, 1.7 mi. S of Rt. 28. From the barrier gate at the entrance to the campground (0 mi.), follow the main campground road 1.5 mi. to the end of the farthest loop. At campsite #87 continue straight ahead, pass another gate for summer traffic, and follow yellow ski markers to a junction at 1.7 mi. The Old Dam nature trail goes L across the fish barrier dam, while the ski route goes R. At 2.1 mi. the ski trail reaches a bridge over Limekiln Creek, and just beyond the bridge it comes to a junction with a trail to the L. This trail is the other end of the nature trail. Continuing on to the R, the trail recrosses the brook at 3.1 mi. and comes to an old snowmobile trail at 3.5 mi., where the ski route jogs R and then L to cross the trail. After crossing another smaller brook, the trail comes to a junction at 3.8 mi., where the point-to-point trip diverges L and the loop goes R.

(The point-to-point variation proceeds generally NW on the flat. Snow vehicle routes confuse the trail somewhat at 5.2 mi., but in general the trail sticks close to the L bank of Third Lake Creek until it reaches a chain barrier at 6.4 mi. From here the road is obvious to South Shore Road at 7.1 mi. This trailhead is 5.5 mi. from the village of Inlet on South Shore Road.)

The more commonly done loop trip, which goes R at 3.8 mi., continues on the flat to the N of Limekiln Swamp and then climbs slightly to a junction at 5.2 mi. (Trail straight ahead leads in 1.4 mi. to Limekiln Rd., 0.7 mi. N of the campground entrance. One can also continue all the way to Inlet via the ski touring center's trails for a total tour of 8.4 mi.) Turning R at this junction at 5.2 mi., the ski route descends to cross the head of Limekiln Swamp, goes over a low ridge, and finally descends to the campground road at 6.8 mi. Turning L, one returns to the starting point at 7.0 mi. **ADK**

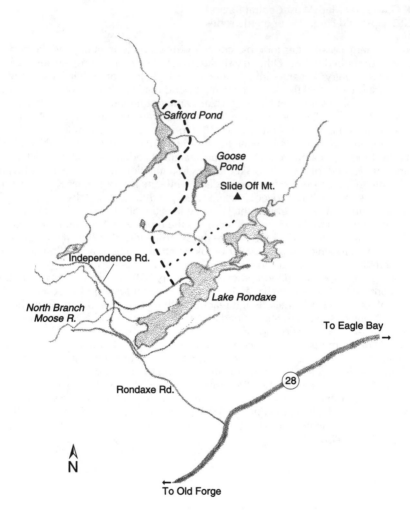

Safford Pond (36)
Based on ADK West-Central Region map

36. SAFFORD POND

Distance: 6.0 mi., round-trip
Difficulty: Novice–Intermediate
ADK Guide and Map: West-Central Region
USGS Maps: Big Moose 15' or Eagle Bay metric series

Although this tour can be done as a 5.2-mi. point-to-point tour, the N end of the trail is rougher and it is a fairly long car shuttle. From the S, the skiing is mostly flat and there is a shorter destination of Goose Pond. Although marked as a snowmobile trail, it receives relatively light use by snow vehicles .

To reach the trailhead, turn W off Rt. 28 onto Rondaxe Rd. between Old Forge and Eagle Bay. At 1.4 mi. along Rondaxe Rd. turn R and then immediately L, and continue to a bridge across the North Branch of the Moose River at 1.9 mi. (Although plowed, this 0.5 mi. of road will likely be snow-covered as this is also a major snowmobile trail.) One hundred yards after this bridge, one turns R on North Rondaxe Rd. and proceeds until there are snowmobile trail markers on the L, 2.6 mi. from Rt. 28.

From the road (0 mi.) the trail is flat to a junction with a more heavily used snowmobile trail leading R to Dart Lake. Bearing L at this junction, the Safford Pond Trail skirts the base of a hill, crosses a wide wet area at 0.4 mi., and continues on the level to a side trail to Goose Pond at 1.3 mi. Beyond this junction, the trail stays on the E edge of the wetland E of Safford Pond to a junction with a side trail L to the pond at 2.7 mi. This side trail leads to the shore of Safford Pond at 3.0 mi.

ADK

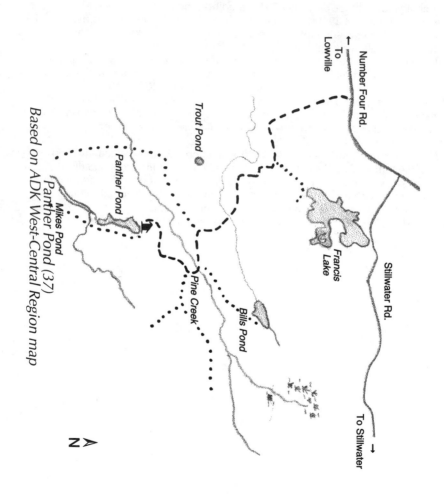

Based on ADK West-Central Region map

Panther Pond (37)

Mikes Pond

N

37. PANTHER POND

Distance: 10.2 mi., round-trip
Difficulty: Intermediate
ADK Guide and Map: West-Central Region
USGS Maps: Number Four 15' or metric series

This remote and seldom visited pond with a lean-to sees a few snowmobilers and fewer skiers, but it is a worthwhile trip with some nice skiing on the usually unplowed Smith Road. Marked as a snowmobile trail, this diverges from Number Four Rd. 0.9 mi. W of the junction with Stillwater Rd. Begin skiing here (0 mi.) up past the former site of the Number Four fire tower and then gently down to a sand pit on the L at 1.5 mi. This is the start of an unmarked trail to Francis Lake. Continuing on, the road swings sharp L at 2.3 mi., where a private road goes straight ahead to Trout Lake, and then continues mostly on the level across Bills Pond outlet at 2.8 mi. before climbing gently to a junction at 3.3 mi. (The trail going R is known as the Panther Pond Loop, but it is a much longer approach to Panther Pond.) Past this junction the road is again level to the summer parking at 3.8 mi. Turning R, the route passes a barricade, crosses Pine Creek, and comes to a junction and register at 4.0 mi. (Trail L is the E end of the Panther Pond Loop.) The direct route to Panther Pond goes R along an old road to a junction at 4.8 mi. The marked route to the lean-to goes L and up over a small hill to the lean-to at 5.1 mi. An unmarked trail leads to the pond as well and is a possible alternate route. **ADK**

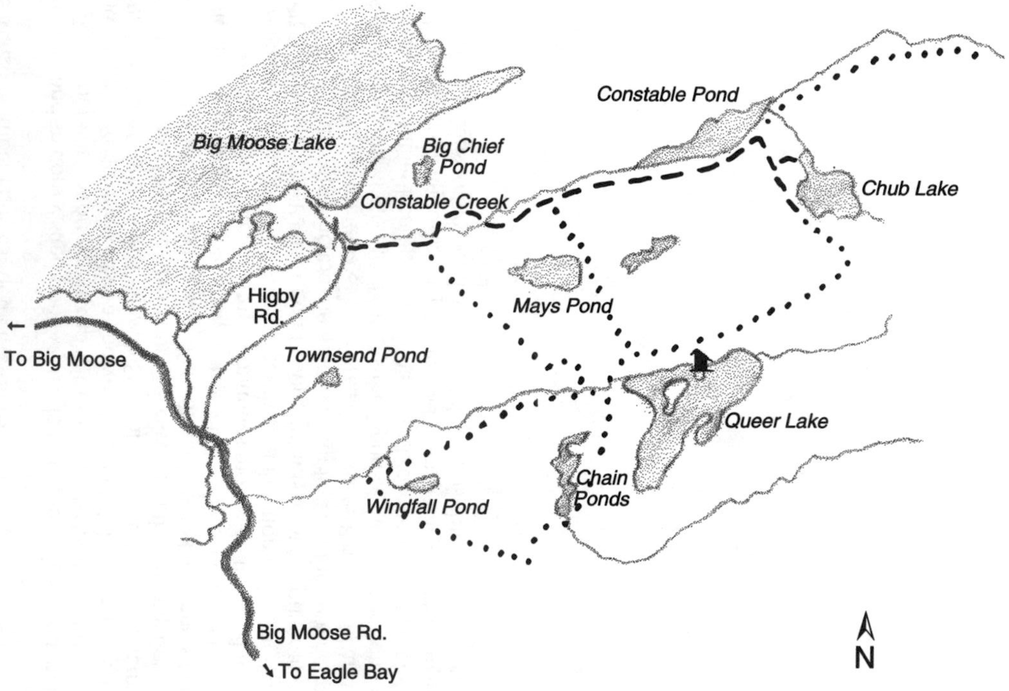

Chub Lake (38)
Based on ADK West-Central Region map

To Big Moose

Big Moose Lake

Higby Rd.

Townsend Pond

Big Moose Rd.

To Eagle Bay

Windfall Pond

Constable Creek

Big Chief Pond

Constable Pond

Mays Pond

Chain Ponds

Queer Lake

Chub Lake

N

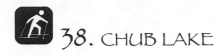

38. CHUB LAKE

Distance: 6.0 mi., round-trip
Difficulty: Intermediate
ADK Guide and Map: West Central Region
USGS Maps: Big Moose 15' or Eagle Bay metric series

Chub Lake is but one of many attractive ponds in the Pigeon Lake Wilderness Area to which one can ski without having to share the trail with snowmobiles. This trip follows the most skiable of the whole network of trails linking Pigeon, Queer and Cascade lakes, and Mays, Chain, and Windfall ponds. (Each of these other trails either has a few steep spots or suffers from lack of maintenance, but all can and have been skied.) This trip is not skied often, so trail breaking may be a consideration.

Starting from Rt. 28 in Eagle Bay, drive 3.8 mi. on Big Moose Rd. and then turn R on Higby Rd. for 1.3 mi. to Judson Rd., a private, unplowed road. There may not be any sign marking Judson Rd., and there are no markers for the first 0.2 mi. After this point there are blue markers. From Higby Rd. (0 mi.) the route follows Judson Rd. for 0.2 mi. and then turns R just before the road turns L to cross Constable Creek. A few yards after this R turn, one comes to a vehicle barrier and register. Then the trail follows an old road along the bank of Constable Creek to a junction at 0.5 mi. with a side trail going R to Queer Lake. Continuing straight ahead 75 yds. beyond this junction, the ski route crosses Constable Creek and then meets a road at 0.9 mi. Turning R on this road,the route soon recrosses Constable Creek on a lumber bridge. Turning L after this bridge, the blue-marked route leaves the road and soon reaches state land.

At 1.3 mi. a side trail to Mays Pond goes R. Continuing straight ahead at this junction, there is a nice stretch of skiing next to the open wetland along Constable Creek. Constable Pond is first visible on the L at 2.2 mi., and a short spur trail diverges L to Constable Pond at 2.5 mi. Fifty yds. beyond this spur trail, the blue-marked trail comes to a junction with a yellow-marked trail leading R to Chub Lake. (Trail straight ahead leads to Pigeon Lake, but recent lack of maintenance makes it a less than perfect trail to ski.) Turning R at the junction, one climbs slightly, descends, and climbs again to a junction at 2.8 mi. To reach Chub Lake, one can either turn L at this junction and follow the trail for 0.2 mi. to the NW shore of the lake; or one can bear R and continue down for 0.2 mi. to a crossing of an inlet to Chub Lake (with the lake clearly visible to the L). With either option one reaches the lake at 3.0 mi. **ADK**

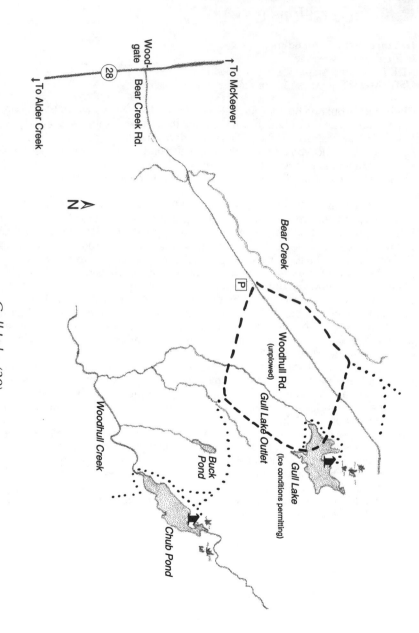

To McKeever

Wood-
gate

28

Bear Creek Rd.

To Alder Creek

N

Bear Creek

P

Woodhull Rd.
(unplowed)

Gull Lake Outlet

Gull Lake
(ice conditions permitting)

Buck
Pond

Woodhull Creek

Chub Pond

Gull Lake (39)
Based on ADK West-Central Region map

39. GULL LAKE

Distance: 6.4–7.3 mi., round-trip
Difficulty: Intermediate
ADK Guide and Map: West-Central Region
USGS Maps: McKeever 15' or metric series

Gull Lake is but one of many possible tours in the Black River Wild Forest, which stretches generally SE from Rt. 28 to Rt. 8 and SW of the extensive holdings of the Adirondack League Club. There are still a number of small private inholdings, and many of the trails are subject to vehicular use. Nevertheless, a quick glance at the map will show that about the only limit to skiing in this area is one's own imagination. Gull Lake is a beautiful destination with a lean-to, and one can return via Chub Pond to make an attractive loop trip.

From Rt. 28 at Woodgate (approx. 17 mi. S of Old Forge) take Bear Creek Rd. 3.0 mi. to a large map and register at the usual end of plowing. From the end of the road (0 mi.) the route to Gull Lake continues on an unplowed road called Woodhull Rd.. At 0.3 mi. the trail to Chub Pond goes R. (This is the return for the possible loop tour.) At 0.4 mi. the yellow-marked trail goes L off Woodhull Rd. (If there is sufficient snow to cover the vehicle ruts, one can ski the road for another 1.6 mi. to the junction with the Gull Lake Trail.)

The yellow-marked hiking trail is nearly level as it roughly parallels Woodhull Rd.. Passing a junction with a side trail L at 1.3 mi., the trail reaches a junction at 2.0 mi. Here the yellow-marked route to Bear Lake and Sand Lake Falls continues straight ahead. Bearing R and up a gentle hill, the red-marked Gull Lake Trail climbs easily to a crossing of Woodhull Rd. at 2.4 mi. (Those who choose to stay on the road should be alert and watch carefully for this crossing.) Beyond Woodhull Rd., the red-marked Gull Lake Trail climbs gradually for another 0.3 mi., after which there is flat skiing to a junction at 3.0 mi. near the shore of Gull Lake. Trail L leads to the lean-to on the N shore of the lake, but if ice conditions permit it is easier to ski down to the lake and across to the lean-to at about 3.2 mi.

If the trailbreaking hasn't been too bad and one wants to see some more terrain, one can return by skiing to the S shore from the lean-to and, after a short bushwhack, picking up the trail to Chub Pond. After finding the marked trail, turn L and head S to a junction with the Chub Pond Trail at 5.7 mi. Turning R, the trail crosses Gull Lake Outlet at 6.2 mi. and reaches Woodhull Rd. at 7.1 mi. The starting point is 0.2 mi. to the L. **ADK**

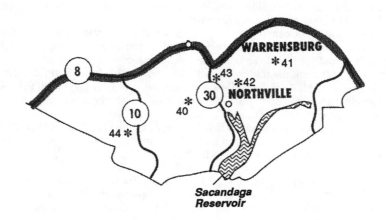

SOUTHERN REGION

Novice–Intermediate
44. Dry and Dexter lakes

Intermediate
40. Rock Lake
41. Lizard Pond and Baldwin Springs from Garnet Lake
43. Murphy Lake from Pumpkin Hollow Road

Intermediate–Expert
42. Wilcox Lake via East Stony Creek

SOUTHERN REGION

Although the southern Adirondacks are accessible to large numbers of potential skiers, there has not been as much ski touring activity here as one might expect. The area from Benson to Piseco and Speculator often has good snow; but for some reason only a few of the tours described here regularly see much skier traffic. The limitation may be that the area's centerpiece, the Silver Lake Wilderness Area, has only the Northville-Placid Trail as a major trail. The adjoining Wilcox Lake, Ferris Lake, and Shaker Mountain Wild Forest Areas have more trails, but most of them are designated snowmobile trails. Not all of these snowmobile trails are heavily trafficked, however, and there are some appealing destinations and some interesting skiing to be discovered beyond the frequently done Rock Lake tour.

Lapland Lake in Benson is the only cross-country ski center in the region, but it is one of the Adirondacks' most established centers with a deserved reputation for consistently having the best snow conditions in the Adirondacks. Piseco and Speculator also maintain small ski loops (permit required), even though snowmobiling is the primary winter recreation in these two towns.

Southern Cross-country Ski Center and Sites
Lapland Lake (518) 863-4974
Speculator/Piseco area (518) 548-4521

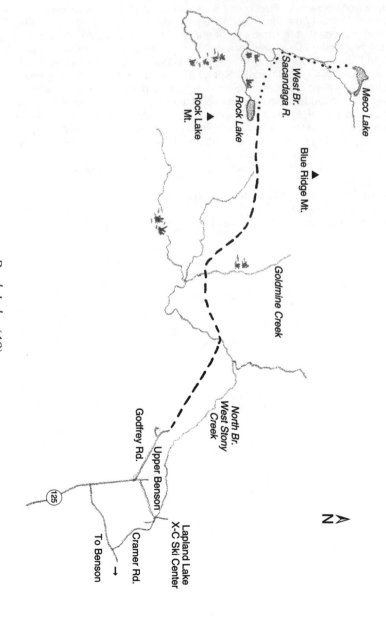

Rock Lake (40)
Based on ADK Southern Region map

West Br.
Sacandaga R.

Meco Lake

Rock Lake

Rock Lake
Mt.

Blue Ridge Mt.

Goldmine Creek

North Br.
West Stony
Creek

Godfrey Rd.

Upper Benson

125

Lapland Lake
X-C Ski Center

Cramer Rd.

To Benson

N

40. ROCK LAKE

Distance: 9.2 mi., round-trip
Difficulty: Intermediate
ADK Guide and Map: Southern Region or Northville-Placid Trail
USGS Maps: Lake Pleasant 15' or Three Ponds Mt. metric series

This is the most popular tour in the region, offering wilderness skiing, an attractive destination, and a nice downhill run on the return. Its proximity to Lapland Lake Cross-country Ski Center provides an option for less ambitious skiers in a group, or an alternative in the event that groomed snow is preferable to the prevailing backcountry conditions. The route is the first part of the 132-mile Northville–Placid (N-P) Trail.

The access is from Rt. 30 between Northville and Wells. Turn onto Benson Rd., marked signs for both the Northville–Placid Trail and Lapland Lake Cross-country Ski Center. At 5.2 mi. a road goes R to Lapland Lake, but bear L. At 5.8 mi. the road crosses an iron bridge over West Stony Creek. Bear R immediately after the bridge, and then at 6.6 mi. bear L onto Godfrey Rd. (The parking lot is on the R, just over 7.0 mi. from Rt. 30.)

From the parking lot (0 mi.), blue DEC markers lead gently down to a trail register on the R. Here the trail goes R on an old woods road and then down to a hunting camp belonging to a fish and game club. This is private property and one must remain on the trail, for which there is a public easement. The trail now climbs gradually and then descends gently to the bank of West Stony Creek at 1.2 mi. Turning L, it passes an old cable barrier and arrives at a bridge over the brook at 1.5 mi. The trail now climbs steadily to a crossing of Goldmine Creek at 2.4 mi. This section of trail is somewhat rocky and eroded and may be rough skiing with marginal snow cover; but after Goldmine Creek the trail improves as it descends a bit before climbing again to a height of land at 3.2 mi. The trail then descends easily, climbs again, and reaches the junction with the side trail to Rock Lake at 4.5 mi. The side trail leads 0.1 mi. L to a small clearing, once the site of a lean-to.

This trip can be extended by about 1.5 mi. by skiing to the W end of Rock Lake and then continuing 0.5 mi. through the marshy area next to the outlet. Then turn R (N) and ski up to the head of a second marshy area. A short bushwhack leads to the N-P Trail. Turning R on the N-P Trail, a ski of just under one mile, brings one back to the junction with the Rock Lake side trail. One can also continue on the N-P Trail to Meco Lake at 6.4 mi. or Silver Lake at 7.3 mi., but there may not be broken track to these more distant destinations. One should be able to return in about two-thirds of the time required to reach any of these destinations, but do make note of any troublesome brook crossings so as to avoid any unpleasant surprises on the return trip. **ADK**

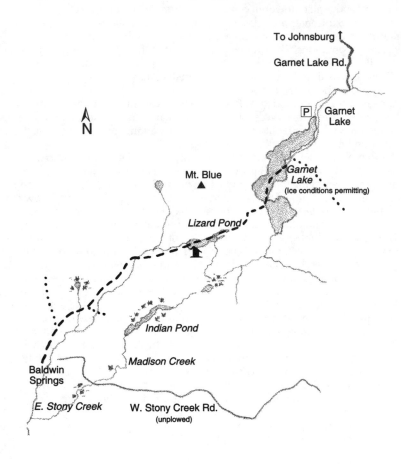

Lizard Pond and Baldwin Springs from Garnet Lake (41)
Based on ADK Southern Region map

41. LIZARD POND AND BALDWIN SPRINGS FROM GARNET LAKE

Distance: 4.5 mi., round-trip to Lizard Lake lean-to; 10.3 mi., round-trip to Baldwin Springs
Difficulty: Intermediate
ADK Guide and Map: Southern Region
USGS Maps: Thirteenth Lake 15' or Bakers Mills metric series

Although most of this tour is flat and relatively easy skiing, the initial 0.5-mi. climb from Garnet Lake to Lizard Pond (misspelled "Lixard" on many maps) requires solid intermediate-level skills to negotiate. This section of trail is also a bit rough and requires a foot or more of solid base before being skiable. Lizard Pond is a particularly attractive destination, while continuing on to Baldwin Springs offers very pleasant skiing through a variety of forest types. Baldwin Springs itself is on a popular snowmobile route between Harrisburg and Route 8, but this particular route via Lizard Pond, although designated as a snowmobile trail, is not often used by vehicles.

The start is a small DEC boat-launching site on Garnet Lake. From Rt. 8 in Johnsburg, take Garnet Lake Rd. approximately 6. 0 mi. SW to a R turn up to the dam at the end of Garnet Lake. From the dam it is 0.9 mi. on a narrow but usually passable road to the parking area at the boat-launching site. From the parking area (0 mi.), ski SW on the lake for 0.7 mi. to the narrowest part of the lake. The trail to Lizard Pond starts on the W shore of Garnet Lake, directly across from the point of the peninsula on the E shore. The trail is marked with snowmobile trail markers but no sign as of 1993.

From the lake, the trail climbs moderately with a few breaks to the E end of the Lizard Pond marsh at 1.3 mi. from the parking area. The trail skirts the S side of the marsh, but the easiest skiing is across the marsh and W across the lake to the lean-to near the W end at 2.0 mi. From here one can see both the nearby rocky slopes of Mt. Blue and the more distant prominence of Crane Mt.

Beyond the end of Lizard Pond the trail is less defined, but the wet areas encountered by summer hikers present little problem to skiers. From the W end of the pond, the trail descends slightly, traverses a small ridge, and then crosses two bridges at 2.6 mi. The trail now turns L and follows down the R bank of the outlet to Lizard Pond. After crossing several more streams, the trail enters a thick stand of tall hemlocks at 3.2 mi. followed by tall pines at 3.5 mi. At 4.4 mi., signs mark the junction with a snowmobile trail leading L to Indian Pond. (This trail is not shown on the ADK hiking map as it is overgrown and crosses too much wet ground to be passable in summer.) Turning R, the trail to Baldwin Springs soon crosses another stream on a good bridge and then passes two enormous glacial erratics on the R.

Beyond these erratics, the character of the land changes as one enters an area of sandy pine barrens. At 4.9 mi. the Lizard Pond Trail reaches a junction with the Bartman Trail coming in from the N past Fish Pond. Turn L and continue for another 0.2 mi. to a bridge over Stony Creek, with the main clearing at Baldwin Springs just beyond at 5.1 mi. Here there is a register and the junction with the well-used Cod Pond snowmobile trail. There was once a short-lived, tiny settlement here in lumbering days, but little now remains. **ADK**

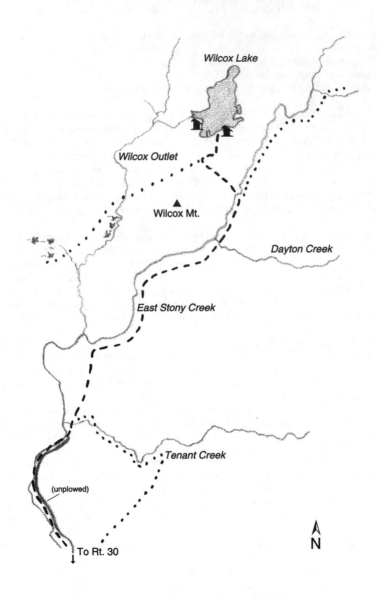

Wilcox Lake via East Stony Creek (42)
Based on ADK Southern Region map

42. WILCOX LAKE VIA EAST STONY CREEK

Distance: 13.4 mi., round-trip
Difficulty: Intermediate–Expert
ADK Guide and Map: Southern Region
USGS Maps: Harrisburg 15' or Hope Falls and Harrisburg metric series

Wilcox Lake is an attractive destination that perhaps attracts too many visitors traveling via too many kinds of conveyances. Erosion by illegal ATVs and dirt bikes has made sections of this route rougher than they otherwise would be, so a foot or more of packed snow is desirable before attempting this tour. The East Stony Creek Trail is also a snowmobile trail, but it is less used as a motorized approach to Wilcox Lake than the approaches from the E or W. While thus perhaps not the ideal ski tour, the ski along East Stony Creek is quite scenic and can be very enjoyable. Furthermore, Wilcox Lake can be very peaceful and beautiful—especially if one is able to ski here on a weekday.

The start is at the end of plowing on Hope Falls Rd., which branches from Old Northville Rd. at the N end of Sacandaga Reservoir. Hope Falls Rd. can be found from Northville or by taking the present Rt. 30 N to its crossing of the Sacandaga River and then turning R (E) for 1.5 mi. to the junction just E of the bridge over East Stony Creek. Hope Falls Rd. is marked with a DEC sign for Wilcox Lake. At 2.6 mi. from Old Northville Rd., bear R and then bear L at 3.2 mi. Plowing ends at 5.9 mi. just after the pavement ends. The trailhead and the trail beyond the end of the road are on private property, so one must stay on the marked trail as requested by numerous signs. The trail is marked with both blue DEC disks and orange snowmobile disks.

From the trailhead (0 mi.) there is a register on the R at 50 yds., followed by a bridge across Tenant Creek at 0.2 mi. The trail now climbs gradually up a valley behind a hill before dropping down to the bank of the creek again at 1.3 mi. Crossing a tributary at 2.1 mi., the trail climbs away from the creek at 2.7 mi., reaches the crest of a ridge at 3.1 mi., and then descends to a crossing of Dayton Creek at 3.6 mi. The trail now becomes rougher up to the Bakertown suspension bridge at 4.2 mi., after which it climbs moderately to the junction with the Willis Lake Trail at 4.9 mi. Bearing R, the trail joins the jeep trail from Harrisburg at 5.0 mi. and then bears L and down to the lean-to on the shore at 5.2 mi. **ADK**

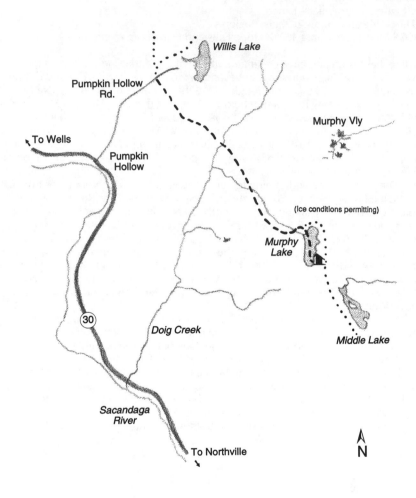

Willis Lake

Pumpkin Hollow
Rd.

Murphy Vly

To Wells

Pumpkin
Hollow

(Ice conditions permitting)

Murphy
Lake

30

Doig Creek

Middle Lake

Sacandaga
River

To Northville

N

Murphy Lake from Pumpkin Hollow Road (43)
Based on ADK Southern Region map

43. MURPHY LAKE FROM PUMPKIN HOLLOW ROAD

Distance: 8.2 mi., round-trip
Difficulty: Intermediate
ADK Guide and Map: Southern Region
USGS Maps: Lake Pleasant and Harrisburg 15′ or Three Ponds Mt. and Hope Falls metric series

Set in a deep valley, Murphy Lake is an attractive destination with a pretty lean-to at its SE corner. The trail has one short steep spot, but otherwise is is quite skiable as it follows the route of an old stagecoach road. As is the case with most of the ski routes in this area, the surface of the trail is somewhat eroded and at least a foot of packed snow is required for good skiing. There is moderate snowmobile traffic on this route.

The start is 1.5 mi. from Rt. 30 near the end of Pumpkin Hollow Rd., which turns E from Rt. 30 0.3 mi. N of the sign designating the town line of Wells. At the start there are DEC signs indicating snowmobile trails heading both left to Pine Orchard and Wilcox Lake and right to Murphy Lake. The trail itself is marked with both yellow DEC and snowmobile trail disks. From the trailhead (0 mi.) the trail descends a short, steep pitch at 0.2 mi. but then is mostly flat to an unmarked junction at 0.9 mi. At this junction the Murphy Lake Trail bears L, followed by another sharp L at 1.1 mi. Soon the trail begins a moderate to steep descent on a washed-out section of old road before leveling out and crossing Doig Creek on a wooden bridge at 1.8 mi. Now the trail climbs gradually to a crossing (no bridge) of the outlet to Murphy Lake at about 2.4 mi. and then follows this stream for a mile to a second crossing—again without benefit of a bridge—at 3.4 mi. In good conditions, neither of these crossings should require more than normal care. (The second crossing is potentially more difficult but can be avoided by skiing up a ridge to the outlet of the pond.)

After the second crossing, the trail proceeds up through a narrow ravine and reaches the W shore of Murphy Lake at 3.8 mi. The attractive lean-to on Murphy Lake is located about 0.3 mi. along the SE shore of the lake. **ADK**

Dry and Dexter lakes (44)
Based on ADK Southern Region map

44. DRY AND DEXTER LAKES

Distance: 5.8 mi., round-trip
Difficulty: Novice–Intermediate
ADK Guide and Map: Southern Region
USGS Maps: Piseco Lake 15' (or Morehouse Mt. metric series) and Canada Lake 7.5'

In addition to the two primary objectives, one can extend this tour with a trip through the marshes connecting Dexter Lake with Spectacle Lake and return via the Spectacle Lake Trail for a round-trip of approximately 8.5 mi. The trail as far as Dry Lake is generally flatter and therefore less eroded than many of the other old roads in this area, making this a good choice if there is less than a foot of packed snow. There is, however, one steeper eroded section getting to Dexter Lake.

The start is on Rt. 10 just past the second bridge over the West Branch of the Sacandaga River N of the hamlet of Arietta. The trailhead is marked with a small DEC sign. From the road (0 mi.) the trail climbs gently and then descends slightly to a crossing of a heavily-used snowmobile trail at 0.5 mi. Beyond the snowmobile trail is a fork. (Trail L leads to Good Luck Lake.) Bearing R, the trail continues gently up and down, reaching a large wet area at 1.2 mi., a stream with an old bridge at 1.4 mi., and finally a view of Dry Pond at 2.1 mi. One can either stick with the trail or descend to the pond and ski to the W end at 2.3 mi. From Dry Pond the trail climbs gradually up into a ravine and then at 2.7 mi. begins to descend a steep, rocky ravine to the shore of Dexter Lake at 2.9 mi.

Snowmobile markers continue beyond. The trail they mark is indistinct in summer, and without any recent snowmobile activity a map and compass is the only realistic method to proceed to Spectacle Lake and the possible round-trip. With recent snowmobile use, however, this route can be followed—using care not to follow just any track so that one will indeed arrive at Spectacle Lake. **ADK**

Norm Landis

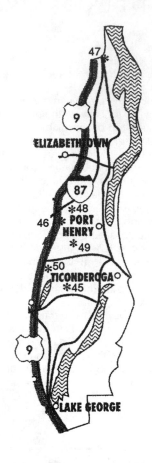

EASTERN REGION

Novice–Intermediate
45. Pharaoh Lake
47. Valcour Island; novice, interior loop; intermediate, perimeter loop.
49. Berrymill and Moose Mountain ponds

Intermediate
46. Round Pond from Sharp Bridge Campsite
48. Crowfoot Pond
50. Crane Pond, Tubmill Marsh, and Lilypad and Rock ponds

EASTERN REGION

Comprised mostly of the terrain east of the Adirondack Northway (I-87), the Eastern Region offers numerous opportunities for shorter tours to a variety of interesting destinations. The most unique tour in the region (and perhaps in all of the Adirondacks) is Valcour Island in Lake Champlain, but there are other more "standard" tours that don't require just the perfect combination of snow and ice conditions that Valcour Island does. The longest tours are in the Pharaoh Lake Wilderness Area, the region's only designated wilderness area.

Probably this region's biggest problem is that sitting on the east edge of mountains, it tends not to receive as much snow as the rest of the Adirondacks. Sometimes a coastal storm will track just right and the Champlain Valley will actually be about the only place to get snow, but usually the eastern Adirondacks has to make do with the "leftovers" of any storm. In a normal to above-average snow year this is not a problem, but some years have seen only a few days of skiable snow in many parts of this region.

There are a few cross-country ski centers in the region where one can call to check on conditions. The Town of Schroon Lake also maintains some cross-country ski trails along with their snowmobile trail system, and the Wooden Ski and Wheel in Plattsburgh is an established and knowledgeable ski shop.

Eastern Cross-country Ski Center and Sites
Ausable Chasm Cross-country Ski Center (518) 834-9990
Schroon Lake (518) 532-7675
Wooden Ski and Wheel Ski Shop, Plattsburgh (518) 561-2790

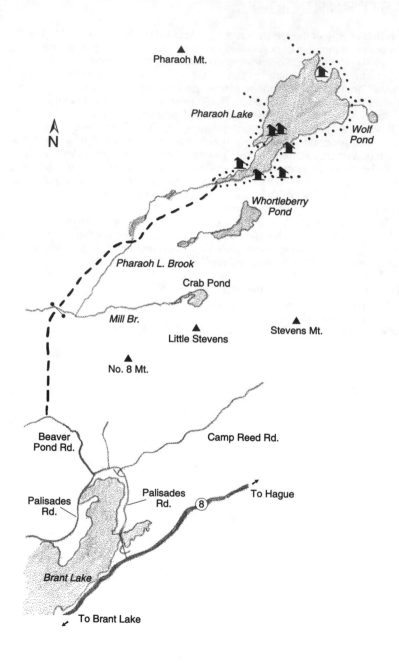

Pharaoh Lake (45)
Based on ADK Eastern Region map

45. PHARAOH LAKE

Distance: 8.2 mi., round-trip to S end of lake; 12.6 mi., round-trip to N end of lake
Difficulty: Novice–Intermediate
ADK Guide and Map: Eastern Region
USGS Maps: Paradox Lake 15' or Pharaoh Mt. 7.5'

This two-mile-long lake with several picturesque lean-tos along its shores is not only beautiful but also may claim the title as the largest Adirondack lake not reached by a road. The approach is via a long-abandoned road so that the skiing is generally easy. The distance to the lake is 1.6 mi. longer in the winter than in summer, but with skiing this nice one should consider an extra 3.2 mi. of skiing a delightful bonus.

To find the start, turn off Rt. 8 onto Palisades Rd. at the E end of Brant Lake (approx. 6 mi. NE of the hamlet of Brant Lake). From Palisades Rd. turn R onto Beaver Pond Rd., which is the third road to the R at 1.5 mi. from Rt. 8. Drive another 1.0 mi. on Beaver Pond Rd. to the unmarked beginning of Pharaoh Lake Road on the R. Pharaoh Lake Rd. may be plowed for the first few hundred yds. to some private camps, but skiers should park on Beaver Pond Rd. since there is no public parking at the end of the plowed section.

From Beaver Pond Rd. (0 mi.), the skiing is nearly level through a notch between Park and No. 8 Mts. to the wide valley of Mill Brook and the summer parking area at 1.6 mi. After crossing Mill Brook on a plank bridge, the trail soon begins to climb. At 2.1 mi. the grade eases, after which gentle ups and downs lead to a bridge across Pharaoh Lake Brook at 2.8 mi. From this bridge the trail climbs briefly and then levels out next to an extensive open area of beaver activity on the L. Continuing generally close to the brook the trail reaches the S end of Pharaoh Lake at 4.1 mi. Although this is a good destination in itself, most skiers will want to ski up the lake to one of the several lean-tos along the shore. One is rewarded with a rapidly widening view of the surrounding mountains the farther one skis up the lake. It is approximately 2.2 mi. more to the lean-to at the N end of the lake. **ADK**

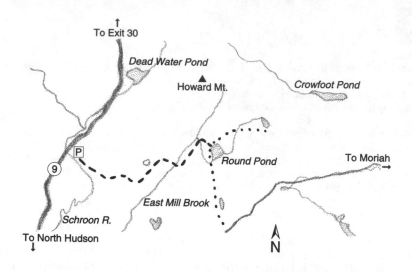

Round Pond from Sharp Bridge Campsite (46)
Based on ADK Eastern Region map

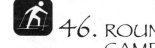46. ROUND POND FROM SHARP BRIDGE
CAMPSITE

Distance: 8 mi., round-trip
Difficulty: Intermediate
ADK Guide and Map: Eastern Region (description only) or High Peaks
USGS Maps: Elizabethtown 15' or Witherbee metric series

The trail to Round Pond from Sharp Bridge has not been maintained as consistently as one might like, but it is still passable; and Round Pond is worth a bit of extra effort to reach. For most of its length this tour follows old wagon roads that were significant transportation links in the early to mid-nineteenth century, even if it is now hard to imagine this often narrow trail as a road. The start is at Sharp Bridge Campground on U.S. Rt. 9, 7.1 mi. N of the hamlet of North Hudson and 2.9 mi. S of Exit 30 on the Northway. There is usually a small parking area plowed on the E side of the highway, but traffic is light on this section of highway and parking on the road should present no problem.

From the road (0 mi.) ski to the far end of the field next to the river and pick up the red-marked trail; this trail follows the L bank of the Schroon River for 0.8 mi. to an old bridge abutment. This was the original crossing of the Schroon River by the Cedar Point Road that by 1830 ran from Port Henry to Newcomb on a line N of the present Blue Ridge Rd. A few years later the Great Northern Turnpike (the predecessor of Rt. 9) began to share this crossing which was used until a bridge was built at the present campground.

At this point, the trail turns sharp L and over a small rise to a potentially difficult crossing of a small brook. Once beyond the brook, the route climbs a moderate grade to a pass at 1.5 mi. after which it drops in two successive pitches to flatter going in a magnificent stand of white pines. Continuing mostly on the flat, the trail arrives at the S end of East Mill Flow at 2.7 mi.

The hiking trail turns R to cross the brook below the flow, but skiers can usually use the ice to cross to the road on the E side or ski up the flow for about 0.7 mi. At 3.4 mi. the outlet of Round Pond crosses the old road and enters East Mill Flow, and just N of this point the road turns sharp R and climbs gently to a junction at 3.5 mi. Here the red-marked hiking trail turns sharp R, but skiers should follow the old road which continues straight ahead. It almost immediately comes within sight of Round Pond. There are some attractive rocks on a point on the N shore, which is reached at 4.0 mi.

From Round Pond, one can continue NE on the old road for about a mile to Moriah Pond and its views of the rugged cliffs of Broughton Ledge. Another possible variation is to ski to the S end of Round Pond and return down the large marsh next to the outlet. The marked hiking trail leads to Trout Pond at the North Hudson-Moriah Rd., but this trail is too rough to be good skiing. **ADK**

Mark Meschinelli

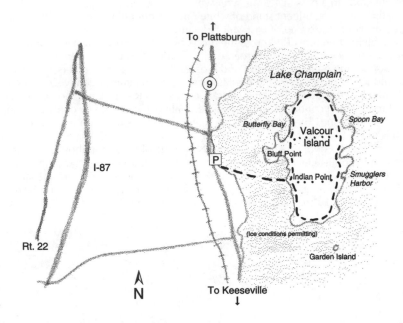

Valcour Island (47)

 47. VALCOUR ISLAND

Distance: 7.7 mi., round-trip on perimeter trail; 5.5 mi., round-trip using both interior trails
Difficulty: Novice (interior loop) to Intermediate (perimeter loop)
ADK Guide and Map: Eastern Region
USGS Maps: Keeseville and Plattsburgh 7.5′

Separated from the mainland by a mile-wide channel, Valcour Island offers a unique and interesting tour when the conditions are right. First, of course, the channel must be sufficiently frozen. This relatively sheltered and shallow channel freezes long before the main lake freezes, but it still may be mid- to late January before it is safe. As soon as it is safe, local ice fishermen will have their shanties on the ice (even vehicles when the ice is thick enough); this is the best indication for visitors that the ice is thick enough. The second ingredient, snow, can in some years be more of a problem, but a call to the Wooden Ski and Wheel bike and ski shop can provide information for the snow on the mainland side of the channel. Even if skimpy snow occasionally forces one to walk, just getting onto this island is a rewarding experience.

Valcour Island is most famous not for its skiing but for the Revolutionary War naval engagement in which the American fleet under the command of Benedict

Arnold did enough damage to the British fleet to delay the planned British invasion from the north by a full year. As a result of this delay, the Americans gained enough strength to later defeat the British at the Battle of Saratoga. In more recent times, visitors to the islands have despaired at the sometimes constant roar of Air Force jets based at Plattsburgh Air Force Base. We can only hope that with the lessening of world tensions there will be fewer aircraft, and thus less noise in the future.

The best start for this trip is at what is variously called Valcour Landing or Peru Docks located on Rt. 9, 3.2 mi. S of the railroad underpass S of Plattsburgh Air Force Base, or 3.3 mi. N of the junction of Rtes. 9 and 442. Rt. 442 is reached from Exit 35 on I-87.

There is plenty of parking, but don't block access to the lake for those who want to drive to their ice-fishing shanties. From the shore, a compass bearing of 114 degrees magnetic takes one to Indian Point, where it is easy to ski up and off the ice. The perimeter trail is located at the top of the meadow. This perimeter trail leads 5.7 mi. around the island with two interior trail permitting shorter loops (see sketch map).

The most spectacular views are from the cliffs at the S end of Valcour Island, found by turning R from Indian Point, but one must also negotiate the toughest skiing on the island to descend the E side of this high headland. (To find an easier interior route, turn L at Indian Point and find the Nomad Trail, which almost immediately goes R and directly across the island to Smuggler's Harbor.)

At Smuggler's Harbor a small iron fence surrounds a bronze plaque with a poem in memory of the captain of the Canadian ship Nomad which was sunk in World War One with the loss of all hands. This cove was apparently a favorite anchorage of the captain in his days as a civilian sailor. Continuing N from Smuggler's Harbor, one passes Sloop Bay and side trails to Paradise and Spoon bays before reaching a junction with the Royal Savage Trail. From here the perimeter trail again has some steeper skiing to get around the N end of the island, past Beauty Bay to a picnic and camping area at Butterfly Bay.

If the skiing isn't too bad on the ice, one can return to the start directly from Butterfly Bay past the prominent 1874 lighthouse on Bluff Point. Otherwise, continue S from Butterfly Bay to either Bullhead Bay or Indian Point and then return across the ice. **ADK**

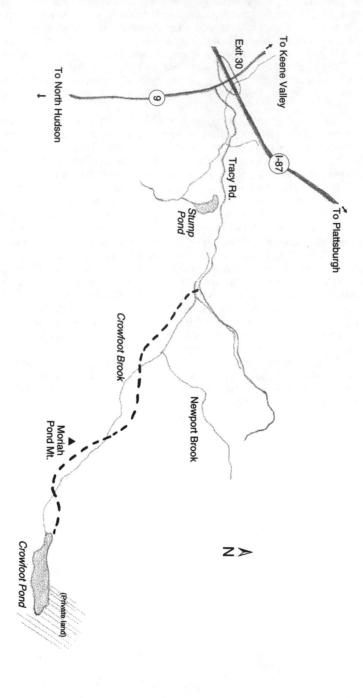

Crowfoot Pond (48)
Based on Mineville and Underwood quadrangles

# 48. CROWFOOT POND

Distance: 5.2 mi., round-trip
Difficulty: Intermediate
ADK Guide and Map: Eastern Region
USGS Maps: Elizabethtown 15' or Witherbee metric series

Although marked as a snowmobile trail, actual vehicular use is not great enough to diminish the pleasure of this short jaunt up to an attractive pond followed by a delightful run back down. From Exit 30 on the Adirondack Northway, go S on Rt. 9 200 yds. and turn L on Tracy Road leading to Mineville, Witherbee, and Moriah. The start of the tour is 1.2 mi. from Rt. 9 where an old road leads R and down toward Crowfoot Brook. One usually will have to park on Tracy Road, finding the straightest and widest spot possible. From the road (0 mi.), the trail goes down 100 yds. and crosses Crowfoot Brook on a good new bridge. Turning L on the other side, the trail climbs to another bridge across Crowfoot Brook at 0.8 mi. after which the climb continues. (The 300-yd.-long downhill approaching the sharp turn across this bridge is the only tricky spot on the return trip.)

At 1.1 mi. the climb eases and the trail begins a short descent. After crossing several small side streams, the trail resumes a gradual climb and recrosses Crowfoot Brook at 1.7 mi. and again at 2.0 mi. Continuing a gradual climb, the trail comes within sight of Crowfoot Pond at 2.5 mi., with open land along the shore reached at approximately 2.6 mi. There are private camps beyond, so this is as good a place as any to turn around and enjoy the coast back to the starting point. **ADK**

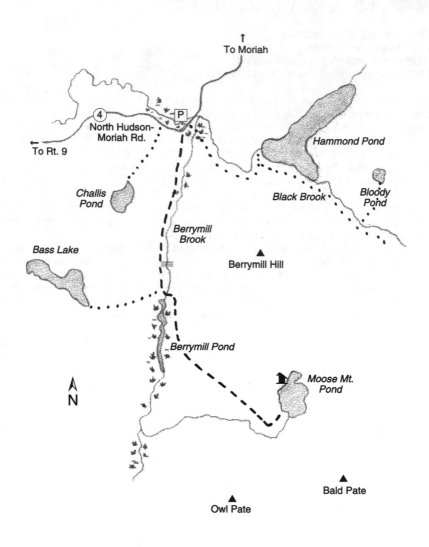

↑
To Moriah

④ North Hudson-
Moriah Rd.

P

Hammond Pond

←
To Rt. 9

Challis
Pond

Black Brook

Bloody
Pond

Bass Lake

Berrymill
Brook

Berrymill Hill ▲

Berrymill Pond

⋏
N

Moose Mt.
Pond

Bald Pate ▲

Owl Pate ▲

Berrymill and Moose Mt. ponds (49)
Based on Paradox Lake quadrangle

49. BERRYMILL AND MOOSE MT. PONDS

Distance: 6.2 mi., round-trip
Difficulty: Novice–Intermediate
ADK Guide and Map: Eastern Region (extension to Moose Mt. Pond is new and therefore not shown on any current topographic map)
USGS Maps: Paradox Lake 15' or 7.5'

The destination in this tour is a virtually unknown pond that recently has been made accessible with the construction of a trail from Berrymill Pond. A new lean-to at the N end of Moose Mountain Pond further enhances the tour. From the lean-to and the low cliffs nearby, one can see Moose Mt. and Owl Pate from a perspective that makes them appear far higher than their low, 2,000-ft elevations would indicate. There is also a possible side trip to Bass Lake and an adjacent tour to Hammond and Bloody ponds to round out the opportunities for short, relatively easy ski trips in this area.

The start for all these trips is on the North Hudson–Moriah Rd., which runs E from Rt. 9, N of North Hudson. Coming from either the N or S on Rt. 9, signs for Moriah and Champlain Bridge direct one onto an old section of Rt. 9 from which the North Hudson–Moriah Rd. branches E. It is 2.9 mi. from this point to the trail-head at a large turnout on the S side of the road. One must be careful as the trail to Challis Pond branches off less than 0.1 mi. before this trail; and the trail to Hammond Pond starts less than 0. 1 mi. E of the Moose Mt. Pond trail. There are presently (1994) no signs for any of these trails, but the Moose Mt. Pond trail is marked with blue DEC disks.

Heading practically due S (as opposed to SE for Hammond Pond), the trail reaches the edge of a marsh at 0.3 mi. A new bypass trail goes R and up, but in winter the best route is to follow the old road through the marsh and then up until the bypass trail returns from the R at 0.7 mi. One now climbs gradually past a small waterfall to a junction with the trail to Bass Lake at 1.3 mi. Bearing L, the trail soon crosses a new bridge over the outlet to Berrymill Pond. (The pond and marsh extend S for about 1.5 mi. and make an interesting side trip.)

After crossing the bridge, one slowly climbs away from the pond, heading SE and finally NE through mature pine and hemlock forests to the S end of Moose Mt. Pond at 2.9 mi. The trail continues along the W shore, but the easiest skiing is across the pond to the lean-to at 3.1 mi. **ADK**

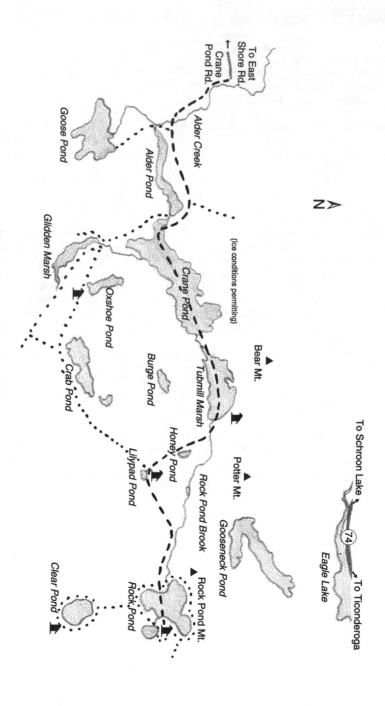

Crane Pond, Tubmill Marsh and Lilypad and Rock ponds (50)
Based on ADK Eastern Region map

To East
Shore Rd.

Crane
Pond Rd.

Alder Creek

Goose Pond

Alder Pond

Glidden Marsh

N

(ice conditions permiting)

Crane Pond

Oxshoe Pond

Burge Pond

Crab Pond

Tubmill Marsh

Bear Mt.

Honey Pond

Lilypad Pond

Potter Mt.

Rock Pond Brook

Gooseneck Pond

To Schroon Lake

74

Eagle Lake

To Ticonderoga

Clear Pond

Rock Pond

Rock Pond Mt.

50. CRANE POND, TUBMILL MARSH, LILYPAD POND AND ROCK POND

Distances: Crane Pond, 3.8 mi. round-trip Tubmill Marsh, 7.6 mi. round-trip
Lilypad Pond, 10.0 mi. round-trip Rock Pond, 13.2 mi. round-trip
Difficulty: Intermediate
ADK Guide and Map: Eastern Region
USGS Maps: Paradox Lake 15′ or Paradox Lake, and Graphite 7.5′

The northern part of the Pharaoh Lake Wilderness Area is characterized by
numerous bodies of water, prolific beaver activity, and many small rocky knobs
with sharp cliffs. Those who make it all the way to Rock Pond will have seen a
good sampling of what this region has to offer without having to negotiate any of
the steep sections that most trails in this area seem to have in one place or another.
By using the low valley of Crane Pond and Tubmill Marsh, this route both avoids
steep climbing and offers many views of the surrounding countryside. One could
do the tour to Rock Pond as an approximate 8 mi. point-to-point trip, coming out at
Putnam Pond; but this does have some steeper skiing at the E end and requires a
fairly long and complicated shuttle. Another possibility is to return via Crab and
Oxshoe ponds to Crane Pond.

From the flashing light at the junction of Rtes. 9 and 74 off Exit 28 in Schroon
Lake, proceed E on Rt. 74 and then turn R on South Rd. about 0.6 mi. after crossing
the Schroon River. In another 0.6 mi. turn L on Alder Meadow Rd. for 0.9 mi., and
then turn L on Crane Pond Rd., which is plowed for another 1.5 mi. At the end of
the road there is supposed to be a barrier preventing all vehicular access since this
is the boundary of the Pharaoh Lake Wilderness Area. A sign still posted as of 1992
gives one opinion of the controversy that resulted in a barrier first being placed and
then removed, followed by a now-famous televised fistfight over just what sort of
access was appropriate. The area is more peaceful now, but it may be some time
before the barrier is replaced.

The skiing starts along the unplowed road from the parking area at the end of
the plowed road (0 mi.). One climbs gently to a bridge over Alder Creek at 0.7 mi.,
and then descends slightly to a junction with a trail R to Goose Pond at 0.9 mi.
Continuing over a ridge and down, the road passes a trail L to Rt. 74 at 1.7 mi. and
reaches the end of the road at Crane Pond at 1.9 mi. From here the route goes onto
the ice of Crane Pond and proceeds to the E end of the pond at 3.0 mi., followed
by a short ski through a marsh to Tubmill Marsh—now a pond in its own right due
to beaver activity. At the E end of Tubmill Marsh at 3.8 mi., one continues E up
Rock Pond Brook to join the trail blue-marked from Eagle Lake at 3.9 mi. Once on
the trail, turn R and climb past much evidence of beaver activity to a junction at
4.8 mi. (Trail straight ahead goes to Crab and Oxshoe ponds.)

Turning L at this junction, one soon comes to a short side trail to a lean-to on
Lilypad Pond, followed by a gradual descent to Rock Pond Brook, which the trail
then follows to Rock Pond at 6.6 mi. There is a lean-to on the E shore past the
small islands in the pond. **ADK**

INDEX

NOTES

Other Publications
of
The Adirondack Mountain Club, Inc.
814 Goggins Road
Lake George, N.Y. 12845-4117
(518) 668-4447

BOOKS

An Adirondack Sampler I, Day Hikes for All Seasons
An Adirondack Sampler II, Backpacking Trips for All Seasons
85 Acres: A Field Guide to the Adirondack Alpine Summits
Adirondack Canoe Waters: North Flow
Adirondack Canoe Waters: South & West Flow
The Adirondack Mt. Club Canoe Guide to Western & Central New York State
Winterwise: A Backpacker's Guide
Climbing in the Adirondacks
Guide to Adirondack Trails: High Peaks Region
Guide to Adirondack Trails: Northern Region
Guide to Adirondack Trails: Central Region
Guide to Adirondack Trails: Northville-Placid Trail
Guide to Adironadack Trails: West-Central Region
Guide to Adirondack Trails: Eastern Region
Guide to Adirondack Trails: Southern Region
Guide to Catskill Trails
Geology of the Adirondack High Peaks Region
The Adirondack Reader
Forests and Trees of the Adirondack High Peaks Region
Our Wilderness: How the People of New York Found, Changed, and Preserved the
Adirondacks
Adirondack Wildguide (distributed by ADK)
Adirondack Park Mountain Bike Preliminary Trail and Route Listing

MAPS

Trails of the Adirondack High Peaks Region
Trails of the Northern Region
Trails of the Central Region
Northville-Placid Trail
Trails of the West-Central Region
Trails of the Eastern Region
Trails of the Southern Region

Price list available on request.